Snell's Equity

SNELL'S EQUITY

FIRST SUPPLEMENT TO THE THIRTY-FOURTH EDITION

JOHN McGHEE QC, MA (Oxon)
of Lincoln's Inn, Barrister

STEVEN ELLIOTT QC, BA (Hons), JD (Hons), DPhil (Oxon)
of Lincoln's Inn, Barrister

CONTRIBUTORS

STUART BRIDGE **MA (Cantab)**
One of Her Majesty's Circuit Judges; Bencher of the Middle Temple; Life Fellow of Queens' College, Cambridge; Law Commissioner for England and Wales 2001–2008

MATTHEW CONAGLEN **LLB (Hons) (Auck), LLM (Mich), PhD (Cantab)**
Professor of Equity and Trusts, University of Sydney; Academic Barrister, New South Wales and Door Tenant at XXIV Old Buildings

PAUL S. DAVIES **MA, PhD (Cantab)**
of Lincoln's Inn, Barrister; Professor of Commercial Law, University College London

SIMON DOUGLAS **DPhil (Oxon)**
Associate Professor of Law, Jesus College, Oxford

DAVID FOX **PhD (Cantab)**
of Lincoln's Inn, Barrister; Professor of Common Law, University of Edinburgh

BEN McFARLANE **MA (Oxon), BCL**
Professor of English Law, University of Oxford; Fellow, St John's College, Oxford

RICHARD NOLAN **MA (Cantab)**;
Professor of Law, University of York; Barrister of the Middle Temple and Door Tenant at Erskine Chambers

JANET O'SULLIVAN **MA, PhD (Cantab)**;
University Senior Lecturer, Faculty of Law, University of Cambridge; Fellow and Director of Studies in Law, Selwyn College, Cambridge

SWEET & MAXWELL

 THOMSON REUTERS

Published and typeset in 2021 by Thomson Reuters,
trading as Sweet & Maxwell
Registered in England & Wales, Company No.1679046.
Registered Office and address for service:
5 Canada Square, Canary Wharf, London E14 5AQ.

For further information on our products and services, visit
www.sweetandmaxwell.co.uk

Printed and bound by CPI Group (UK) Ltd, Croydon, CR0 4YY

A CIP catalogue record for this book is available from the British Library.

ISBN (print): 978-0-414-08373-8

ISBN (e-book): 978-0-414-08375-2

ISBN (print and ebook): 978-0-414-08374-5

TITLE HISTORY

First Edition	(1868) by Edmund Henry Turner Snell
Thirty-Fourth Edition	(2020) by J. A. McGhee and S. Elliott
First Supplement to the Thirty-Fourth Edition	(2021) by J. A. McGhee and S. Elliott

PREFACE

We are sad to have to record the death of Stuart Bridge in September this year. As one our long standing contributors who joined the team for the 32nd Edition in 2010 we greatly valued his insights and guidance. He will be sorely missed.

We are delighted to welcome two new contributors. Dr Simon Douglas brings to bear his expertise in trusts, beginning in this supplement with a reworking of Chapter 27, "Appointment, Retirement and Removal of Trustees". Dr Magda Raczynska's will contribute her expertise in securities by assuming responsibility at the next Supplement for Chapter 40, "Floating Charges".

John McGhee QC
Steven Elliott QC

September 2020

PREFACE

HOW TO USE THIS SUPPLEMENT

This is the First Supplement to the Thirty Fourth Edition of *Snell's Equity* and has been compiled according to the structure of the main volume.

At the beginning of each chapter of this Supplement, a mini table of contents of the sections in the main volume has been included. Where a heading in this table of contents has been marked with a square pointer ■, this indicates that there is relevant information in this Supplement to which the reader should refer.

Within each chapter, updating information is referenced to the relevant paragraph in the main volume

This Supplement is up-to-date to 15 September 2020.

TABLE OF CONTENTS

PART II—MAXIMS AND DOCTRINES

PART III—EQUITABLE PROTECTION

PART IV—EQUITABLE REMEDIES

SUPPLEMENTARY TABLE OF CASES

SUPPLEMENTARY TABLE OF STATUTES

(References are to paragraph numbers)

SUPPLEMENTARY TABLE OF STATUTORY INSTRUMENTS

(References are to paragraph numbers)

CHAPTER 5.

THE MAXIMS OF EQUITY

Replace n.9 with:

[9] See, e.g. *Holiday Inns v Broadhead* (1974) 232 E.G. 951, 1087 (Ch), where the maxim that "equity is equality" was used in order to assist a court in deciding how best to give effect, in practice, to a right of B's arising through proprietary estoppel (or, on another view, under a constructive trust: see, e.g. *Cobbe v Yeoman's Row Management Ltd* [2008] UKHL 55; [2008] 1 W.L.R. 1752 at 24 and 31, per Lord Scott). See too *Ball v Ball* [2020] EWHC 1020 (Ch) at [24], and *MV Productions Ltd v Telegraph Media Group* [2020] EWHC 1357 (Ch) at [62] per HHJ Hodge QC: "[I]t is still one of the maxims of equity that 'equity does not act in vain'; and that broad, underlying principle is relevant when the court is called upon to exercise an equitable, remedial discretion."

5-001

1. EQUITY WILL NOT SUFFER A WRONG TO BE WITHOUT A REMEDY

After "abstraction, it is", delete of limited practical use and add:
rarely applied directly.[11a]

5-002

[11a] In *Lehtimaki v Cooper* [2020] UKSC 33, Lady Arden at [144] held that, given that the "facts and circumstances of this case are most unusual", the lack of a previous case in which a court had ordered a fiduciary to cast his vote in a particular way at a company meeting did not prevent a court's making such an order: "ubi jus ibi remedium is one of the maxims of equity and certainly examples can be found where the courts have made directions as to consequential relief in charity cases...". Note that, as explained by Kiefel CJ, Bell and Keane JJ in *Smethurst v Commissioner of Police* [2020] HCA 14, 376 ALR 575 (High Court of Australia), the maxim that equity will not suffer a wrong to be without a remedy "has never meant that the courts of equity would invent a remedy solely because the plaintiff has suffered an injustice for which no remedy was available. A 'wrong' refers to conduct which is recognised as being contrary to law. The maxim means no more than that the court would afford a remedy for the invasion of a subsisting legal or equitable right."

6. HE WHO COMES INTO EQUITY MUST COME WITH CLEAN HANDS

Replace n.42 with:

5-010   [42] The majority in *Patel v Mirza* [2016] UKSC 42; [2017] A.C. 467 thus rejected the "mechanical" approach to the application of the clean hands maxim in *Tinsley v Milligan* [1994] 1 A.C. 340 HL, but supported the result in that case: see Lord Toulson at [112] and Lord Neuberger at [181]. Lord Neuberger at [151] and [171] also supported the result in *Tribe v Tribe* [1996] Ch. 107 CA as consistent with a general rule (identified at [145]) that a claim is permitted where money has been paid "pursuant to a contract to carry out an illegal activity and the illegal activity is not in the event proceeded with owing to matters beyond the control of either party". ". For discussion of the application of the *Patel v Mirza* approach in this context, see e.g. R Nwabueze, 'Illegality and Trusts: Trusts-creating Primary Transactions and Unlawful Ulterior Purposes' [2019] Conv 29.

Replace n.48 with:

[48] For academic consideration of the impact of *Patel v Mirza* in equity, see N. McBride, "The Future of Clean Hands" and P. S. Davies, "Illegality in Equity" in P. S. Davies et al (eds) *Defences in Equity* (Hart, 2018); and P. S. Davies, "Ramifications of Patel v Mirza in the Law of Trusts" in S Green & A Bogg (eds) *Illegality After Patel v Mirza* (Hart, 2018); R Nwabueze, 'Illegality and Trusts: Trusts-creating Primary Transactions and Unlawful Ulterior Purposes' [2019] Conv 29. For a wider consideration of the relationship between the clean hands maxim and the illegality doctrine, see I. Samet, *Equity: Conscience Goes to Market* (OUP, 2018), Ch.4; and also T.L. Anenson, *Judging Equity: The Fusion of Unclean Hands in US Law* (CUP, 2019).

7. DELAY DEFEATS EQUITIES, OR, EQUITY AIDS THE VIGILANT AND NOT THE INDOLENT

Replace first paragraph with:

5-011   This maxim must also be treated with caution. It can be seen as underpinning, in a general sense, the doctrine of laches,[56] which acts as a bar to equitable relief. That doctrine is not based, however, on the mere fact of delay.[57] Something more than mere delay, more even than extremely lengthy delay,[58] is required before B will be denied equitable rights under the doctrine of laches,[59] as the question is whether the lapse of time has given rise to circumstances that now mean it would not be inequitable to deny relief to B. The principal example occurs where, perhaps as a result of having relied on a mistaken belief that B has no relevant right, A would now suffer an irreversible detriment, as a result of B's delay, if B were permitted relief.[60] The doctrine will therefore apply if the delay has resulted in the destruction or loss of evidence by which B's claim might have been resisted,[61] or if B can be said to have released or abandoned any right.[62] There can be no abandonment of a right without full knowledge, legal capacity and free will, so that ignorance or disability or undue influence will be a satisfactory explanation of delay.[63] Laches is also a personal disqualification and will not bind successors in title,[64] although if the circumstances are such as to give rise to a contract between A and B, or a proprietary estoppel based on B's acquiescence, a third party may be bound.[65]

[56] For a discussion of the technical meaning of the term (pronounced "laitches"), see *Partridge v Partridge* [1894] 1 Ch. 351 at 359, 360; J. Brunyate, *Limitation of Actions in Equity* (London: Stevens & Sons, 1932), p.188. In *FMX Food Merchants Import Export Co Ltd v Revenue and Customs Commissioners* [2020] UKSC 1, Lord Briggs at [39], citing this paragraph, confirmed that laches "relates to the pursuit of equitable relief" and so is not available more broadly in relation to other claims.

[57] See e.g. *Re Eustace* [1912] 1 Ch. 561; *Weld v Petre* [1929] 1 Ch. 33 CA; *Rochefoucauld v Boustead* [1897] 1 Ch. 16 CA; *Lazard Bros & Co Ltd v Fairfield Properties Co (Mayfair) Ltd, The Times,* 13 October 1977; *Jones v Stones* [1999] 1 W.L.R. 1739 CA; *Terceira v Terceira* [2011] SC (Bda) 6 Civ; (2010) 13 I.T.E.L.R. 717, where the claimant's unreasonable delay did not lead to laches as it caused no prejudice to the defendants. See also the cogent discussion in *Western Areas Exploration Pty Ltd v Streeter No.3* [2009] W.A.S.C. 213, 431–454. cf. *P & O Nedlloyd BV v Arab Metals Co* [2006] EWCA Civ 1717; [2007] 1 W.L.R. 2288 at 2312 [61] leaving this point open. Note that delay by itself may of course trigger the application of a statutory limitation period.

[58] *Burroughs v Abott* [1922] 1 Ch. 86 (12 years), *Weld v Petrie* [1929] 1 Ch. 33 CA (26 years). In *Cenac v Schafer* [2016] UKPC 25 at [31], it is stated by Sir Kim Lewison that: "in order to resist a claim for specific performance on the ground of delay, it is necessary to show that prejudice has resulted from the delay". See too the discussion at para.17-044 as to the effect of delay in the particular context of applications for specific performance.

[59] As noted by Judge Simon Baker QC in *Mills v Partridge* [2020] EWHC 2171 (Ch) at [117], citing this paragraph. As a result, great caution must be used when considering broad statements such as that of Lord Camden LC in *Smith v Clay* (1767) 3 Bro.C.C. 639n. at 640n: a court of equity "has always refused its aid to stale demands, where a party has slept upon his right and acquiesced for a great length of time. Nothing can call forth this court into activity, but conscience, good faith, and reasonable diligence; where these are wanting, the Court is passive, and does nothing".

[60] This formulation was relied on by Picken J in *Avonwick Holdings Ltd v Azitio Holdings Ltd* [2020] EWHC 1844 (Comm) at [875]. See, e.g. *Fisher v Brooker* [2009] UKHL 41; [2009] 1 W.L.R. 1764, 1781 at 64, per Lord Neuberger: "some sort of detrimental reliance is usually an essential ingredient of laches".

[61] *Reimers v Druce* (1857) 23 Beav. 145 CA; *Bourne v Swan & Edgar Ltd* [1903] 1 Ch. 211 at 219, 220. As confirmed in *Fernandes v Fernandes* [2015] EWHC 814 (Ch) at [67], however, the doctrine will not apply simply because of the death of individuals whose value as potential witnesses is "pure speculation".

[62] *Allcard v Skinner* (1887) 36 Ch. D. 145; *Butlin-Sanders v Butlin* (1985) 15 Fam. Law 126. For the relationship between laches and acquiescence, see para.18–041.

[63] See *Rees v De Bernardy* [1896] 2 Ch. 437 at 445; *Allcard v Skinner* (1887) 36 Ch. D. 145 CA; *Beale v Kyte* [1907] 1 Ch. 564. *Labrouche v Frey* [2016] EWHC 268 (Ch) is an example of acquiescence preventing a challenge to fees paid to trustees where the applicants had for a long period had knowledge, and the means of obtaining knowledge, of the fees (see [320]).

[64] *Nwakobi v Nzekwu* [1964] 1 W.L.R. 1019.

[65] See, e.g. *MEPC Ltd v Christian-Edwards* [1978] Ch. 281 CA at 293. For discussion of the circumstances in which a proprietary estoppel claim may bind a third party, see para.12-052.

9. EQUITY LOOKS TO THE INTENT RATHER THAN TO THE FORM

Replace n.90 with:

[90] "A contract is undoubtedly construed alike both in equity and at law": *Parkin v Thorold* (1852) 16 **5-013**
Beav. 59 at 66–67, per Romilly MR. The contrary view of Harman J in *Smith v Hamilton* [1951] Ch. 174 was rightly described by the editors of *Meagher, Gummow and Lehane's Equity Doctrines and Remedies*, 4th edn (Australia: LexisNexis, 2002) at 3-170 as "nonsense". For further consideration of the importance of form in equity, see e.g. B McFarlane, 'Form and Substance in Equity' in A Robertson & J Goudkamp (eds) *Form and Substance in the Law of Obligations* (Hart, 2019).

10. EQUITY LOOKS ON AS DONE THAT WHICH OUGHT TO BE DONE

Replace n.105 with:

[105] This point was cited with approval by Bell, Keane, Nettle and Edelman JJ in *Commissioner of State* **5-015**
Revnue v Rojoda Pty Ltd [2020] HCA 7, 376 ALR 378 (High Court of Australia) at [47]. Those judges held at [48] that the Western Australian Court of Appeal had misapplied the maxim as it had applied it in a manner which was "unnecessary to give effect to any right or duty recognised by equity". It is possible that the distinction between moral and legal obligations was not given sufficient weight in *Pennington v Waine* [2002] EWCA Civ 227, as the grounds for which A came under a duty to B were not adequately identified (it may be that B's reliance on A's gratuitous promise was crucial, but the point was not fully analysed by the Court of Appeal).

12. EQUITY ACTS IN PERSONAM

(b) Application of the maxim today: Jurisdiction over property abroad.

Replace n.135 with:

[135] See, e.g. P. Birks, "In rem or in personam? Webb v Webb" (1994) 8 *Trusts Law International* 99; **5-019**
A. Briggs, *The Conflict of Laws*, 4th edn (Oxford: OUP, 2019), p.59.

CHAPTER 7.

FIDUCIARIES

1. FIDUCIARIES AND FIDUCIARY RELATIONSHIPS

2. Fiduciary Relationships

(c) Ad hoc fiduciary relationships.

(1) Principles.

Replace second paragraph with:

7-005   There is, however, growing judicial support for the view that:

> "a fiduciary is someone who has undertaken to act for or on behalf of another in a particular matter in circumstances which give rise to a relationship of trust and confidence."[36]

The undertaking can be implied in the circumstances, particularly where someone has taken on a role in respect of which fiduciary duties are appropriate.[37] Hence, it has been said that:

> "fiduciary duties are obligations imposed by law as a reaction to particular circumstances of responsibility assumed by one person in respect of the conduct or the affairs of another."[38]

> "The concept encaptures a situation where one person is in a relationship with another which gives rise to a legitimate expectation, which equity will recognise, that the fiduciary will not utilise his or her position in such a way which is adverse to the interests of the principal."[39]

[36] *Bristol & West Building Society v Mothew* [1998] Ch. 1 at 18; *Lehtimaki v Cooper* [2020] UKSC 33 at [44]; *Arklow Investments Ltd v Maclean* [2000] 1 W.L.R. 594 at 598–600; *Peskin v Anderson* [2000] EWCA Civ 326 at [34]; *Hooper v Gorvin* [2001] W.T.L.R. 575 at 590; *Kyrris v Oldham* [2003] EWCA Civ 1506 at [142]; *Maclean v Arklow Investments Ltd* [1998] 3 N.Z.L.R. 680 at 691 and 723; *Button v Phelps* [2006] EWHC 53 (Ch) at [58]–[61]; *Australian Securities and Investments Commission v Citigroup Global Markets Australia Pty Ltd (No.4)* [2007] FCA 963 at [272]; (2007) 160 F.C.R. 35; *South Australia v Peat Marwick Mitchell & Co* (1997) 24 A.C.S.R. 231, 265; *Schipp v Cameron* [1998] NSWSC 997 at [697]; *Galambos v Perez* [2009] SCC 48; [2009] 3 S.C.R. 247; *Grimaldi v Chameleon Mining NL (No.2)* [2012] FCAFC 6 at [177]; (2012) 200 F.C.R. 296; *McWilliam v Norton Finance (UK) Ltd* [2015] EWCA Civ 186 at [40]-[42], [2015] 1 All E.R. (Comm.) 1026; *FHR European Ventures LLP v Cedar Capital Partners LLC* [2014] UKSC 45 at [5]; [2015] A.C. 250; *Farrar v Miller* [2018] EWCA Civ 172 at [75]; *Sheikh Tahnoon v Kent* [2018] EWHC 333 (Comm) at [158]-[159].

[37] *Vivendi SA v Richards* [2013] EWHC 3006 (Ch) at [139]–[141].

[38] *F & C Alternative Investments (Holdings) Ltd v Barthelemy (No.2)* [2011] EWHC 1731 (Ch) at [225]; [2012] Ch. 613.

[39] *Arklow Investments Ltd v Maclean* [2000] 1 W.L.R. 594 at 598; *Lehtimaki v Cooper* Lehtimäki v Cooper [2020] UKSC 33 at [47]-[49] and [91]; *Farrar v Miller* [2018] EWCA Civ 172 at [75]. See also *Waxman v Waxman* (2004) 7 I.T.E.L.R. 162 at [512] Ont CA; *Brandeis Brokers Ltd v Black* [2001] 2 All E.R. (Comm) 980 at [36]–[37]; *Hughes Aircraft Systems International v Airservices Australia* (1997) 146 A.L.R. 1 (FCA) at 81; *News Ltd v Australian Rugby Football League Ltd* (1996) 64 F.C.R. 410 at 541; *Australian Securities Commission v AS Nominees Ltd* (1995) 62 F.C.R. 504 at 521; (1995) 133 A.L.R. 1 (FCA) at 17; *Glandon Pty Ltd v Strata Consolidated Pty Ltd* (1993) 11 A.C.S.R. 543 at 557 (NSWCA); *Australian Securities and Investments Commission v Citigroup Global Markets Australia Pty Ltd (No.4)* [2007] FCA 963 at [273]; (2007) 160 F.C.R. 35; *Brooker v Friend* [2006] NSWCA 385 at [149]; *John Youngs Insurance Services Ltd v Aviva Insurance Service UK Ltd* [2011] EWHC 1515 (TCC) at [94(3)]; *F & C Alternative Investments (Holdings) Ltd v Barthelemy (No.2)* [2011] EWHC 1731 (Ch) at [223] and [225]; [2012] Ch. 613; *Grimaldi v Chameleon Mining NL (No.2)* [2012] FCAFC 6 at [177]; (2012) 200 F.C.R. 296. This stems from Paul Finn's academic work: see Finn, *"The Fiduciary Principle"* in Equity, Fiduciaries and Trusts (1989) 1 at 54; P. Finn, "Fiduciary Law and the Modern Commercial World" in E. McKendrick (ed), *Commercial Aspects of Trusts and Fiduciary Obligations* (Oxford: Clarendon Press, 1992) 7 at 8.

Replace n.41 with:

[41] *Vivendi SA v Richards* [2013] EWHC 3006 (Ch) at [139] and [142]; *Tan Yok Koon v Tan Choo Suan* [2017] SGCA 13 at [194] and [199]; [2017] 1 SLR 654..

Replace n.42 with:

[42] *New Zealand Netherlands Society "Oranje" Inc v Kuys* [1973] 1 W.L.R. 1126 at 1130. See also *Lehtimäki v Cooper* Lehtimäki v Cooper [2020] UKSC 33 at [51] and [101]; *Breen v Williams* (1996) 186 C.L.R. 71 at 107–108; *Maruha Corp v Amaltal Corp Ltd* [2007] NZSC 40 at [21]–[22]; [2007] 3 N.Z.L.R. 192; *Australian Securities and Investments Commission v Citigroup Global Markets Australia Pty Ltd (No.4)* [2007] FCA 963 at [285]; (2007) 160 F.C.R. 35; *John Youngs Insurance Services Ltd v Aviva Insurance Service UK Ltd* [2011] EWHC 1515 (TCC) at [94(6)], [96].

Replace n.49 with:

[49] See also *John Alexander's Clubs Pty Ltd v White City Tennis Club Ltd* (2010) 241 C.L.R. 1 at [90] and [101]; [2010] HCA 19; *Adventure Golf Systems Australia Pty Ltd v Belgravia Health & Leisure Group Pty Ltd* [2017] VSCA 326 [125]–[126]; (2017) 54 V.R. 625.

(2) Examples.

Replace n.64 with:

[64] See, e.g. *Global Container Lines Ltd v Bonyad Shipping Co (No.1)* [1998] 1 Lloyd's Rep. 528 at 546– **7-006** 547; *Button v Phelps* [2006] EWHC 53 (Ch) at [59]–[61]; *Ross River Ltd v Cambridge City Football Club Ltd* [2007] EWHC 2115 (Ch) at [197]; *Gibson Motorsport Merchandise Pty Ltd v Forbes* [2006] FCAFC 44 at [2]; (2006) 149 F.C.R. 569; *John Alexander's Clubs Pty Ltd v White City Tennis Club Ltd* [2010] HCA 19 at [44]; (2010) 241 C.L.R. 1; *Farrar v Miller* [2018] EWCA Civ 172 at [75]; *Adventure Golf Systems Australia Pty Ltd v Belgravia Health & Leisure Group Pty Ltd* [2017] VSCA 326 at [134]; (2017) 54 V.R. 625; and see *Explora Group Plc v Hesco Bastion Ltd* [2005] EWCA Civ 646 at [51], citing this paragraph.

2. GENERAL NATURE OF FIDUCIARY DUTIES

Replace n.74 with:

[74] *Securities & Exchange Commission v Chenery Corp* 318 U.S. 80 at 85–86; 87 L. Ed. 626 at 632 **7-007** (1943); quoted with approval in *Re Goldcorp Exchange Ltd (In Receivership)* [1995] 1 A.C. 74 at 98. See also *Boardman v Phipps* [1967] 2 A.C. 46 at 127; *Lehtimäki v Cooper* [2020] UKSC 33 at [35].

1. Loyalty

Replace first paragraph with:

"The distinguishing obligation of a fiduciary is the obligation of loyalty. The **7-008** principal is entitled to the single-minded loyalty of his fiduciary."[76] This obligation of loyalty has several facets, which are addressed separately below. Millett LJ provided a non-exhaustive list of those facets in his judgment in *Bristol & West Building Society v Mothew*, which is "widely regarded as a masterly survey of the modern law of fiduciary duties"[77]:

> "A fiduciary must act in good faith; he must not make a profit out of his trust; he must not place himself in a position where his duty and his interest may conflict; he may not act for his own benefit or the benefit of a third person without the informed consent of his principal."[78]

The fundamental fiduciary obligation of loyalty comprises two related themes.[79] The first prohibits a fiduciary from acting in a situation where there is a conflict between the fiduciary's duty and his or her interest: "the objective is to preclude the fiduciary from being swayed by considerations of personal interest".[80] The second prohibits a fiduciary from making a profit out of his or her fiduciary position: "the objective is to preclude the fiduciary from actually misusing his position for his personal advantage".[81] It has been suggested that the second of these two themes is merely an instance of the first.[82] In most cases where the profit theme applies, the fundamental conflict theme will also capture the situation and give rise to liability on the part of the fiduciary.[83] The profit theme developed out of the conflict theme,[84] but has reached the point where it applies without the need for any conflict analysis.[85] In other words, the two principles largely overlap but there may be cases where the two do not necessarily both apply.[86]

[76] *Bristol & West Building Society v Mothew* [1998] Ch. 1 at 18; *Boulting v Association of Cinematograph, Television & Allied Technicians* [1963] 2 Q.B. 606 at 636; *KLB v British Columbia* [2003] 2 S.C.R. 403; (2003) 230 D.L.R. (4th) 513 at [48]; *Chirnside v Fay* [2004] 3 N.Z.L.R. 637 at [51]; *Sinclair Investment Holdings SA v Versailles Trade Finance Ltd* [2005] EWCA Civ 722 at [20]; *Ultraframe (UK) Ltd v Fielding* [2005] EWHC 1638 (Ch) at [1285]–[1288]; *Gibson Motorsport Merchandise Pty Ltd v Forbes* [2006] FCAFC 44 at [11]; (2006) 149 F.C.R. 569; *Stevens v Premium Real Estate Ltd* [2009] NZSC 15 at [67]; [2009] 2 N.Z.L.R. 384; *Sinclair Investments (UK) Ltd v Versailles Trade Finance Ltd* [2010] EWHC 1614 (Ch) at [26]; *Rossetti Marketing Ltd v Diamond Sofa Co Ltd* [2012] EWCA Civ 1021 at [20]; *Adventure Golf Systems Australia Pty Ltd v Belgravia Health & Leisure Group Pty Ltd* [2017] VSCA 326 at [124]; (2017) 54 V.R. 625..

[77] *Johnson v EBS Pensioner Trustees Ltd* [2002] EWCA Civ 164 at [37].

[78] *Bristol & West Building Society v Mothew* [1998] Ch. 1 at 18.

[79] *Australian Securities and Investments Commission v Citigroup Global Markets Australia Pty Ltd (No.4)* [2007] FCA 963 at [291]; (2007) 160 F.C.R. 35; *South Australia v Peat Marwick Mitchell & Co* (1997) 24 A.C.S.R. 231, 264; *Sinclair Investments (UK) Ltd v Versailles Trade Finance Ltd* [2010] EWHC 1614 (Ch) at [29]; *Grimaldi v Chameleon Mining NL (No.2)* [2012] FCAFC 6 at [178]; (2012) 200 F.C.R. 296; *Ancient Order of Foresters in Victoria Friendly Society Ltd v Lifeplan Australia Friendly Society Ltd* [2018] HCA 43 at [67]–[69]; (2018) 265 C.L.R. 1.

[80] *Chan v Zacharia* (1984) 154 C.L.R. 178 at 198 (quoted with approval in *Don King Productions Inc v Warren* [2000] Ch. 291 at [40]).

[81] *Chan v Zacharia* (1984) 154 C.L.R. 178 at 199 (quoted with approval in *Don King Productions Inc v Warren* [2000] Ch. 291 at [40]).

[82] See, e.g. *Broughton v Broughton* (1855) 5 De G.M. & G. 160 at 164 (43 E.R. 831 at 833); *Bray v Ford* [1896] A.C. 44 at 51; *Boardman v Phipps* [1967] 2 A.C. 46 at 123; *New Zealand Netherlands Society "Oranje" Inc v Kuys* [1973] 1 W.L.R. 1126 at 1129; *Ratiu v Conway* [2005] EWCA Civ 1302 at [59]; *Huntington Copper & Sulphur Co (Ltd) v Henderson* (1877) 4 S.C. (4th Series) 294 at 299; *FHR European Ventures LLP v Cedar Capital Partners LLC* [2014] UKSC 45 at [5]; [2015] A.C. 250.

[83] See, e.g. *Boston Deep Sea Fishing & Ice Co v Ansell* (1888) 39 Ch. D. 339 at 355, 357.

[84] See generally A. McClean, "The Theoretical Basis of the Trustee's Duty of Loyalty" (1969) 7 Alberta L. Rev. 218.

[85] See, e.g. *Re Lewis* (1910) 103 L.T. 495; *Regal (Hastings) Ltd v Gulliver* [1967] 2 A.C. 134n. at 144–145, 153, 159; *Brown v Inland Revenue Commissioners* [1965] A.C. 244 at 256, 265; *Boardman v Phipps* [1967] 2 A.C. 46 at 100–101, 103, 105, 118; *Queensland Mines Ltd v Hudson* (1978) 18 A.L.R. 1 at 4.

[86] *Oceanic Life Ltd v HIH Casualty & General Insurance Ltd* [1999] NSWSC 292 at [42].

2. Concurrency of Fiduciary and Non-Fiduciary Duties

Replace n.90 with:

7-009   [90] *Re Goldcorp Exchange Ltd (In Receivership)* [1995] 1 A.C. 74 at 98. See also *Lehtimaki v Cooper* [2020] UKSC 33 at [46]; *Ratiu v Conway* [2005] EWCA Civ 1302 at [71]–[72]; *Strother v 3464920 Canada Inc* [2007] SCC 24 at [141]; [2007] 2 S.C.R. 177; *John Youngs Insurance Services Ltd v Aviva Insurance Service UK Ltd* [2011] EWHC 1515 (TCC) at [94(7)].

4. Proscriptive Duties

Replace n.99 with:

7-011   [99] *Attorney General v Blake* [1998] Ch. 439 at 455; *Breen v Williams* (1996) 186 C.L.R. 71 at 95, 113 & 137–138; *Pilmer v Duke Group Ltd (In Liquidation)* [2001] HCA 31 at [74], [127]; (2001) 207 C.L.R. 165; *Youyang Pty Ltd v Minter Ellison Morris Fletcher* [2003] HCA 15 at [41]; (2003) 212 C.L.R. 484; *Aequitas v AEFC* [2001] NSWSC 14; (2001) 19 A.C.L.C. 1,006 at [284]; *Australian Securities and*

Investments Commission v Citigroup Global Markets Australia Pty Ltd (No.4) [2007] FCA 963 at [290]; (2007) 160 F.C.R. 35; *Brooker v Friend* [2006] NSWCA 385 at [26]; *Gibson Motorsport Merchandise Pty Ltd v Forbes* [2006] FCAFC 44 at [12]; (2006) 149 F.C.R. 569; *P & V Industries Pty Ltd v Porto* [2006] VSC 131 at [32]–[34], [43]; (2006) 14 V.R. 1; *Commonwealth Oil & Gas Co Ltd v Baxter* [2009] CSIH 75 at [14]; *Eric Preston Pty Ltd v Euroz Securities Ltd* [2010] FCA 97 at [428]–[429]; *Grimaldi v Chameleon Mining NL (No.2)* [2012] FCAFC 6 at [178]; (2012) 200 F.C.R. 296; *Howard v Commissioner of Taxation* [2014] HCA 21 at [31], [56]; (2014) 253 C.L.R. 83; *Moulin Global Eyecare Holdings Ltd v Mei* [2014] 17 H.K.C.F.A.R. 466 at [36]; *Ancient Order of Foresters in Victoria Friendly Society Ltd v Lifeplan Australia Friendly Society Ltd* [2018] HCA 43 at [67]; (2018) 265 C.L.R. 1. cf. *Fassihi v Item Software (UK) Ltd* [2004] EWCA Civ 1244 at [41]; *Sharp v Blank* [2015] EWHC 3220 (Ch) at [23]. See further, Conaglen, *Fiduciary Loyalty: Protecting the Due Performance of Non-Fiduciary Duties* (2010) Ch.7.

5.   Scope and Duration of Fiduciary Duties

(a)   Scope.

Replace n.100 with:

[100] *Hospital Products Ltd v United States Surgical Corp* (1984) 156 C.L.R. 41 at 102; *Re Coomber* [1911] 1 Ch. 723 at 729; *New Zealand Netherlands Society "Oranje" Inc v Kuys* [1973] 1 W.L.R. 1126 at 1130; *Lac Minerals Ltd v International Corona Resources Ltd* (1989) 61 D.L.R. (4th) 14 at 28; *Kelly v Cooper* [1993] A.C. 205 at 214; *Henderson v Merrett Syndicates Ltd* [1995] 2 A.C. 145 at 206; *Clay v Clay* [2001] HCA 9 at [46]; *Strother v 3464920 Canada Inc* [2007] SCC 24 at [118], [141]; [2007] 2 S.C.R. 177; *Australian Securities and Investments Commission v Citigroup Global Markets Australia Pty Ltd (No.4)* [2007] FCA 963 at [288]; (2007) 160 F.C.R. 35; *South Australia v Peat Marwick Mitchell & Co* (1997) 24 A.C.S.R. 231 at 266; *Stevens v Premium Real Estate Ltd* [2009] NZSC 15 at 23; [2009] 2 N.Z.L.R. 384; *John Alexander's Clubs Pty Ltd v White City Tennis Club Ltd* [2010] HCA 19 at [91]–[92]; (2010) 241 C.L.R. 1; *Eric Preston Pty Ltd v Euroz Securities Ltd* [2010] FCA 97 at [425]–[426]; *Customer Systems Plc v Ranson* [2012] EWCA Civ 841 at [25]–[29]; *Lehtimaki v Cooper* [2020] UKSC 33 at [79]. Thus, e.g. in the case of an agent employed under a contract, the scope of any fiduciary duties of the agent will be determined by reference to the terms of the underlying contract: *John Youngs Insurance Services Ltd v Aviva Insurance Service UK Ltd* [2011] EWHC 1515 (TCC) at [94(1)].

7-012

(b)   Duration.

Replace n.110 with:

[110] *Ex p. James* (1803) 8 Ves. 337 at 352 (32 E.R. 385 at 390–391); *Re Boles and British Land Co's Contract* [1902] 1 Ch. 244 at 246–247; *Island Export Finance Ltd v Umunna* [1986] B.C.L.C. 460 at 476; *Edmonds v Donovan* [2005] VSCA 27 [56]–[57] and [60]–[61], (2005) 12 V.R. 513

7-013

6.   Authorisation

(a)   Principal's consent.

Replace n.134 with:

[134] *McWilliam v Norton Finance (UK) Ltd* [2015] EWCA Civ 186 at [51]-[54], [2015] 1 All E.R. (Comm.) 1026. See also *Farah Constructions Pty Ltd v Say-Dee Pty Ltd* [2007] HCA 22 at [107]–[108]; (2007) 230 C.L.R. 89; *Australian Securities and Investments Commission v Citigroup Global Markets Australia Pty Ltd (No.4)* [2007] FCA 963 at [296]; (2007) 160 F.C.R. 35. Both of these latter cases involved sophisticated principals: cf. the facts in *Maguire v Makaronis* (1997) 188 C.L.R. 449. See also *Medsted Associates Ltd v Canaccord Genuity Wealth (International) Ltd* [2019] EWCA Civ 83; [2019] 1 W.L.R. 4481, which again involved experienced investors.

7-015

Replace n.138 with:

[138] *FHR European Ventures LLP v Mankarious* [2011] EWHC 2308 (Ch) at [81]–[82]; *McWilliam v Norton Finance (UK) Ltd* [2015] EWCA Civ 186 at [54], [201] 1 All E.R. (Comm.) 1026.

3. CONFLICTS BETWEEN DUTY AND INTEREST

1. General Principle

Replace n.156 with:

7-018   [156] *Bray v Ford* [1896] A.C. 44 at 51; *Australian Securities and Investments Commission v Citigroup Global Markets Australia Pty Ltd (No.4)* [2007] FCA 963 at [313]; (2007) 160 F.C.R. 35.

2. Authorisation

Replace n.179 with:

7-019   [179] *Australian Securities and Investments Commission v Citigroup Global Markets Australia Pty Ltd (No.4)* [2007] FCA 963 at [293]; (2007) 160 F.C.R. 35. See also *Downes v Grazebrook* (1817) 3 Mer. 200 at 208 (36 E.R. 77 at 80).

4. CONFLICTS BETWEEN DUTY AND DUTY

2. Application

(a)   Potential conflict.

Replace third paragraph with:

7-037   Notwithstanding the potential conflict rule, "a director is at liberty to become a director of a rival company, provided that he or she does not make use of confidential information".[373] The correctness of this proposition has been doubted,[374] but it is important that it be recognised that "[a]t most [it] means that the mere fact of being the director of a company will not preclude the director from engaging in a competing business on his or her own account. But it leaves open any issues of actual conflict, or of conflict reasonably perceived to be within the range of sensible possibilities, arising on the facts of a particular case".[375] A close examination of the director's functions and responsibilities in the company is thus required.[376]

[373] *Bell v Lever Bros Ltd* [1932] A.C. 161, 195; *London & Mashonaland Exploration Co v New Mashonaland Exploration Co* [1891] W.N. 165; *In Plus Group Ltd v Pyke* [2002] EWCA Civ 370 at [72]; [2002] 2 B.C.L.C. 201; *Australian Careers Institute Pty Ltd v Australian Institute of Fitness Pty Ltd* [2016] NSWCA 347 at [134]; (2016) 340 A.L.R. 580.

[374] *In Plus Group Ltd v Pyke* [2002] EWCA Civ 370 at [79]–[88]; [2002] 2 B.C.L.C. 201 per Sedley LJ, although see at [75] per Brooke LJ and at [93] per Jonathan Parker LJ; *Scottish Co-operative Wholesale Society Ltd v Meyer* [1959] A.C. 324 at 368; *Commonwealth Oil & Gas Co Ltd v Baxter* [2009] C.S.I.H. 75 at [4]–[5] and [76]–[77]; Beck, "The Quickening of Fiduciary Obligation: Canadian Aero Services v O'Malley" (1975) 53 Can. Bar Rev. 771, 789–791; Christie, "The Director's Fiduciary Duty not to Compete" (1992) 55 M.L.R. 506. See also *Re Thomson* [1930] 1 Ch. 203.

[375] *Links Golf Tasmania Pty Ltd v Sattler* [2012] FCA 634 at [564], (2012) 213 F.C.R. 1. See also *Australian Careers Institute Pty Ltd v Australian Institute of Fitness Pty Ltd* [2016] NSWCA 347 at [4]; (2016) 340 A.L.R. 580.

[376] *Australian Careers Institute Pty Ltd v Australian Institute of Fitness Pty Ltd* [2016] NSWCA 347 at [136]; (2016) 340 A.L.R. 580.

Replace n.378 with:

[378] *Commonwealth Oil & Gas Co Ltd v Baxter* [2009] CSIH 75 at [4]; *Australian Careers Institute Pty Ltd v Australian Institute of Fitness Pty Ltd* [2016] NSWCA 347; (2016) 340 A.L.R. 580.

6. REMEDIES FOR BREACH OF FIDUCIARY DUTY

2. Rescission

Replace n.518 with:

518 *Hurstanger Ltd v Wilson* [2007] 1 W.L.R. 2351 at [43]–[51] (the plaintiff was awarded an account).   **7-053**
And see *Johnson v EBS Pensioner Trustees Ltd* [2002] Lloyd's Rep. P.N. 309. See also *Ross River Ltd
v Cambridge City Football Club Ltd* [2007] EWHC 2115 (Ch) at [203]; *Northampton Regional Livestock
Centre Co Ltd v Cowling* [2014] EWHC 30 (QB) at [188]–[191]; *Medsted Associates Ltd v Canaccord
Genuity Wealth (International) Ltd* [2019] EWCA Civ 83; [2019] 1 W.L.R. 4481; and para.15-016.

3. Account of Profits

(a)   Availability.

Replace n.534 with:

534 *Ancient Order of Foresters in Victoria Friendly Society Ltd v Lifeplan Australia Friendly Society Ltd*   **7-054**
[2018] HCA 43 at [70]; (2018) 265 C.L.R. 1.

Replace n.539 with:

539 *Mahesan S/O Thambiah v Malaysia Government Officers' Cooperative Housing Society Ltd* [1979]
A.C. 374 at 381 and 383; *Armagas Ltd v Mundogas SA* [1986] A.C. 717 at 743; *Fyffes Group Ltd v
Templeman* [2000] 2 Lloyd's Rep. 643 at 660. The payment of a secret commission by a lender to a bor-
rower's broker may also render the relationship between the lender and the borrower unfair for the
purposes of s.140A of the Consumer Credit Act 1974: *Wood v Commercial First Business Ltd* [2019]
EWHC 2205 (Ch) at [148].

Change title of paragraph:

(b)   Fashioning the account.542

542 Part of this paragraph was cited with approval by Vos J in *Bank of Ireland v Jaffery* [2012] EWHC   **7-055**
1377 (Ch) at [291]. See also M. Conaglen "*Identifying the Profits for Which a Fiduciary Must Account*" [2020] C.L.J. 38.

Replace n.545 with:

545 *Ancient Order of Foresters in Victoria Friendly Society Ltd v Lifeplan Australia Friendly Society Ltd*
[2018] HCA 43; 2018) 265 C.L.R. 1.

Replace n.547 with:

547 *Ultraframe (UK) Ltd v Fielding* [2005] EWHC 1638 (Ch) at [158]; *Gamatronic (UK) Ltd v Hamilton*
[2017] B.C.C. 670 at [188]; *Keystone Healthcare Ltd v Parr* [2019] EWCA Civ 1246 at [18]; [2019] 4
W.L.R. 99.

Replace fourth paragraph with:

Thus, where the profit is made out of a business, rather than a specific asset, given
the risks inherent in business activities and the amount of time, effort and skill
required to make a business successful, a principal will not necessarily be awarded
an account of the entire profits of the business.554 It remains of first importance, in
such cases, "to ascertain precisely what it was that was acquired in consequence of
the fiduciary's breach of duty".555 Thus, where the profit has been generated by carv-
ing out the busines of the principal, the fiduciary is more likely to be required to
account for the entire profit of the new business555a but where a company manager
set up his own business and deprived the company of a lucrative agency but the new
business was also based on contributions other than the business connections of the
principal company, the company was awarded an account of the profits of the
manager's new business but only for a period of two years.556 This is based on the

understanding that:

> "given the property in question is the goodwill of the company's business, there will in all probability come a time when it can safely be said that any future profits of the new business will be attributable not to the goodwill misappropriated from the claimant company when the new business was set up but rather to the defendants' own efforts in carrying on that business."[557]

Similarly, a fiduciary who has acted in breach of fiduciary duty, and against whom an account of profits is ordered, may nevertheless be given an allowance for skill and effort employed in obtaining the profit which he has to disgorge,[558] where:

> "it would be inequitable now for the beneficiaries to step in and take the profit without paying for the skill and labour which has produced it."[559]

This power is exercised sparingly, out of concern not to encourage fiduciaries to act in breach of fiduciary duty.[560] It will not likely be used where the fiduciary has been involved in surreptitious dealing or has acted dishonestly or in bad faith.[561] However, allowances are not ruled out simply because the fiduciary can be criticised in the circumstances,[562] and there are instances of them being made even where the fiduciary has acted surreptitiously and deceitfully.[563]

[554] See, e.g. *Clegg v Edmondson* (1857) 8 De G.M. & G. 787 at 814–815 (44 E.R. 593 at 604); *Re Jarvis (Deceased)* [1958] 1 W.L.R. 815 at 821; *Warman International Ltd v Dwyer* (1995) 182 C.L.R. 544 at 560–561.

[555] *Warman International Ltd v Dwyer* (1995) 182 C.L.R. 544 at 565. For an example of directions given as to accounts where a licence was obtained in breach of fiduciary duties owed to former partners, see *John Taylors v Masons* [2001] EWCA Civ 2106 at [37]; [2005] W.T.L.R. 1519.

[555a] See, e.g., *Ancient Order of Foresters in Victoria Friendly Society Ltd v Lifeplan Australian Friendly Society Ltd* [2018] HCA 43 at [4], [8], [10], [16, [17]]; (2018) 265 C.L.R. 1. And see the analysis in M. Conaglen, *"Identifying the Profits for which a Fiduciary Must Account"* [2020] C.L.J. 38, 53-56.

[556] *Warman International Ltd v Dwyer* (1995) 182 C.L.R. 544.

[557] *Murad v Al-Saraj* [2005] EWCA Civ 959 at [115]; [2005] W.T.L.R. 1573.

[558] See, e.g. *Brown v Litton* (1711) 1 P. Wms. 140 at 142 (24 E.R. 329 at 329); *Lord Provost of Edinburgh v Lord Advocate Ex p. Mclaren* (1879) 4 App.Cas. 823 at 839; *Boardman v Phipps* [1967] 2 A.C. 46 at 104, 112; *O'Sullivan v Management Agency & Music Ltd* [1985] 1 Q.B. 428 at 459, 468 and 472; *Warman International Ltd v Dwyer* (1995) 182 C.L.R. 544 at 568; *Badfinger Music v Evans* [2001] W.T.L.R. 1; *Lindsley v Woodfull* [2004] EWCA Civ 720; [2004] 2 B.C.L.C. 131 at [6], [8]; *Re Macadam* [1946] Ch. 73, 82–83; *Cook v Collingridge* (1823) Jac. 607, 623; *Brown v de Tastet* (1821) Jac. 284 at 294, 298 and 299.

[559] *Phipps v Boardman* [1964] 1 W.L.R. 993 at 1018. See also *Accidia Foundation v Simon C Dickinson Ltd* [2010] EWHC 3058 (Ch) at [94]–[95].

[560] *Guinness Plc v Saunders* [1990] 2 A.C. 663 at 701. cf. *Mid-City Skin Cancer & Laser Centre v Zahedi-Anarak* [2006] NSWSC 844 at [273].

[561] *Phipps v Boardman* [1965] Ch. 992 at 1021; *Crown Dilmun v Sutton* [2004] EWHC 52 (Ch) at [213].

[562] *O'Sullivan v Management Agency & Music Ltd* [1985] Q.B. 428 at 468.

[563] *Murad v Al-Saraj* [2005] EWCA Civ 959 at [88]; [2005] W.T.L.R. 1573. See also *Say-Dee Pty Ltd v Farah Constructions Pty Ltd* [2005] NSWCA 309 at [252], although on appeal it was held that no breach of fiduciary duty had been committed: *Farah Constructions Pty Ltd v Say-Dee Pty Ltd* [2007] HCA 22; (2007) 230 C.L.R. 89.

Replace fifth paragraph with:

The fiduciary bears the onus of convincing the court that an accounting of his or her entire profits is inappropriate in the circumstances.[565] It is not relevant in that regard for the fiduciary to argue that the principal would have consented to the profit, had he been asked: such considerations can be relevant to the question whether *the principal* has suffered any loss as a result of the breach of fiduciary duty, but they are not relevant in determining what profit has been made by *the fiduciary* without authorisation and thus in breach of fiduciary duty.[566] It is that profit for which the fiduciary must account, rather than any profit over and above a hypothetical level to which his principal might potentially have agreed. In this sense, the relevant question is not whether the breach of fiduciary duty caused the profit to be made, but rather whether there is a reasonable connection between the breach of duty and the profit.[566a] The liability is focused more on the fact that making and retaining the profit is itself the breach of fiduciary duty, than on whether the breach caused a profit to be made; although the two questions are bound up together in the sense that it is only a breach to make or retain a profit from assets held in a fiduciary capacity, or otherwise generated within the scope of, or by reason of, the fiduciary position, or in a transaction that involved a conflict between duty and interest. This is the relevant "sufficient connection" between the breach of fiduciary duty and the profit which is stripped.

[565] *Warman International Ltd v Dwyer* (1995) 182 C.L.R. 544 at 561–562; *Harris v Digital Pulse Pty Ltd* [2003] NSWCA 10 at [336]; *Ancient Order of Foresters in Victoria Friendly Society Ltd v Lifeplan Australia Friendly Society Ltd* [2018] HCA 43 at [17]; (2018) 265 C.L.R. 1.

[566] *Regal (Hastings) Ltd v Gulliver* [1967] 2 AC 134n., 144-145; *Murad v Al-Saraj* [2005] EWCA Civ 959 at [67], [136]; [2005] W.T.L.R. 1573; *Keystone Healthcare Ltd v Parr* [2019] EWCA Civ 1246 at [15], [2019] 4 W.L.R. 99; *Gray v New Augarita Porcupine Mines Ltd* [1952] 3 D.L.R. 1 at 15 (PC). See also *United Pan-Europe Communications NV v Deutsche Bank AG* [2000] 2 B.C.L.C. 461 at [47]. cf. *Strother v 3464920 Canada Inc* [2007] SCC 24 at [152]–[158]; [2007] 2 S.C.R. 177.

[566a] *Keystone Healthcare Ltd v Parr* [2019] EWCA Civ 1246 at [16]-[18], [2019] 4 W.L.R. 99. See also M. Conaglen "*Identifying the Profits for Which a Fiduciary Must Account*" [2020] C.L.J. 38, esp. at pp. 57-62.

5. Equitable Compensation for Loss

(b) Causation.

Replace n.600 with:

[600] See, e.g. *Satnam Investments Ltd v Dunlop Heywood & Co Ltd* [1999] 3 All E.R. 652 at 668; *Nationwide Building Society v Balmer Radmore* [1999] Lloyd's Rep. P.N. 241 at 278; *Murad v Al-Saraj* [2005] EWCA Civ 959 at [110], [120]; [2005] W.T.L.R. 1573; *Aequitas v AEFC* [2001] NSWSC 14; (2001) 19 A.C.L.C. 1,006 at [443]–[448]; *Edmonds v Donovan* [2005] V.S.C.A. 27 at [78] (2005) 12 V.R. 513. It may also be necessary to consider how third parties would have acted vis-a-vis the principal if there had been no breach of fiduciary duty: see *Nicholls v Michael Wilson and Partners Ltd* [2012] NSWCA 383.

7-059

(d) Interest.

After "a compound basis.", add:

The rate of interest must be suited to the economic realities of the times, which can render older decisions less useful as guides, and courts seek a suitable proxy rate for the general characteristics of the claimant that is being awarded equitable compensation.[623a]

7-061

[623a] *Watson v Kea Investments Ltd* [2019] EWCA Civ 1759 at [71]-[74]; [2019] 4 W.L.R. 145.

6. Forfeiture of Fees

Replace second paragraph with:

If a fiduciary acts dishonestly he will forfeit his right to fees paid or payable by the principal (as distinct from sums paid by a third party, such as a briber).[627] He will also forfeit his right to such fees if he takes a secret profit from a third party

7-062

which is directly related to performance of the duties in respect of which the fees were payable by the principal,[628] even if the principal has benefited from the fiduciary's performance of those duties.[629] Where the breach lies in a failure to pass on relevant information, rather than the taking of a secret profit, the fiduciary will not forfeit his right to fees unless he acted dishonestly or in bad faith.[629a] And, a fiduciary's fees may not be forfeit if the betrayal of trust has not been in respect of the entire subject-matter of the fiduciary relationship and where forfeiture would be disproportionate and inequitable.[630]

[627] See, e.g. *Andrews v Ramsay* [1903] 2 K.B. 635 at 638; *Hippisley v Knee Brothers* [1905] 1 K.B. 1 at 8; *Ian Scott & Co v Medical Installations Co Ltd* (1981) 258 E.G. 556; *Robinson Scammell & Co v Ansell* [1985] 2 E.G.L.R. 41 at 43–44; *Kelly v Cooper* [1993] A.C. 205 at 216; *Stevens v Premium Real Estate Ltd* [2009] NZSC 15 at [89]; [2009] 2 N.Z.L.R. 384.

[628] *Hippisley v Knee Brothers* [1905] 1 K.B. 1 at 8 & 9; *Price v Metropolitan House Investment & Agency Co (Ltd)* (1907) 23 T.L.R. 630 at 631; *Imageview Management Ltd v Jack* [2009] EWCA Civ 63 at [44] and [46]; *Stupples v Stupples & Co (High Wycombe) Ltd* [2012] EWHC 1226 (Ch) at [21] and [56]; *Avrahami v Biran* [2013] EWHC 1776 (Ch) at [339].

[629] *Rhodes v Macalister* (1923) 29 Com. Cas. 19 at 27; *Imageview Management Ltd v Jack* [2009] EWCA Civ 63 at [47]–[50]; *Rahme v Smith & Williamson Trust Corp Ltd* [2009] EWHC 911 (Ch) at [140]–[141].

[629a] *ACLBDD Holdings Ltd v Staechelin* [2019] EWCA Civ 817 at [81]-[82] and [91] (reported in part, but not this part, at [2019] 3 All E.R. 429).

[630] *Bank of Ireland v Jaffery* [2012] EWHC 1377 (Ch) at [371]–[373].

CHAPTER 8.

FRAUD, UNDUE INFLUENCE AND UNCONSCIONABLE TRANSACTIONS

2. ACTUAL FRAUD

2. The Test for Actual Fraud

Replace n.28 with:

[28] *Arkwright v Newbold* (1881) 17 Ch. D. 310 at 320, per Cotton LJ. See too *Standard Chartered Bank v Pakistan National Shipping Corp (No.2)* [1998] 1 Lloyd's Rep. 684 at 704, per Cresswell J; cited with approval in *Niru Battery Manufacturing Co v Milestone Trading Ltd* [2003] EWCA Civ 1443: "The tort of deceit involves a false representation made by the defendant, who knows it to be untrue, or who has no belief in its truth, or who is reckless as to its truth. If the defendant intended that the plaintiff should act in reliance on such representation and the plaintiff in fact does so, the defendant will be liable in deceit for the damage caused". For further detail as to the tort, see M. Jones et al (eds) *Clerk & Lindsell on Torts*, 23rd edn (Sweet & Maxwell, 2020), Ch.17.

8-007

3. Undue Influence

2. The Test for Undue Influence

(a) A unitary doctrine.

Replace n.63 with:

8-014   63 See the survey and analysis provided by K. Lewison, "Under the Influence" [2011] *Restitution Law Review* 1. For the different argument that the mixed origins of the undue influence authorities mean attempts to reduce it to a core principle are doomed to fail, see R. Honey, "Deconstructing the Equitable Doctrine of Undue Influence: Insights from a Genealogy" (2020) 14 J Eq 58.

(e) Undue influence exercised by a third party.

Replace first paragraph with:

8-019   As noted at para.8-011, if B is induced by the undue influence of a third party (X) to make a gift to A, then relief may be available against A, even if A had no knowledge or notice of the undue influence when acquiring the gift.[88] The remedies available to B will however be limited if A, before acquiring any such knowledge or notice, disposed of the gift or otherwise changed his or her position in good faith. If B instead enters a contract with A as a result of X's undue influence, and X was not acting as B's agent,[89] then B will only be entitled to set the contract aside if A, at the time of the entry into the contract, had actual or constructive notice of X's undue influence.[90] Constructive notice can be shown if A is put on inquiry as to the possibility of X's influence and then fails to take reasonable steps to be satisfied that B's consent to the transaction had been properly obtained.[91] If A is a bank or creditor, and B is standing as surety for the debts of another, A will be put on inquiry whenever the relationship between the surety and the debtor is non-commercial[92]: an obvious example consists of a spouse or partner consenting to the charging of his or her property in order to secure a debt owed by that other partner, or by a company.[93]

[88] See, e.g. *Bridgeman v Green* (1757) Wilmot 58, 97 E.R. 22; *Huguenin v Baseley* (1807) 14 Ves. 273, T 300; 33 E.R. 526, at 536; *Jennings v Cairns* [2003] EWCA Civ 1935.

[89] See para.37-025. Beyond the surety context, see e.g. *O'Sullivan v Management Agency Ltd* [1985] Q.B. 428 CA, where X was an agent of A, the company with whom B entered into a contract.

[90] *Barclays Bank Plc v O'Brien* [1994] 1 A.C. 180 at 195–196; and *Etridge* at [34]–[43] and [139]–[150].

[91] *O'Brien* [1994] 1 A.C. 180 at 196; and *Etridge* at [38].

[92] *Etridge* [82]–[89] esp. [87].

[93] *Etridge* [44]–[49] and [109]. See e.g. *Syndicate Bank v Dansingani* [2019] EWHC 3439 (Ch) at [27], finding that A was put on inquiry where a spouse gave a personal guarantee for a loan to a company, even though the spouses had an equal shareholding in the company and were both directors of it. HHJ Dight there cited with approval the analysis in this work.

Replace n.104 with:

[104] As suggested by J. Cartwright, *Misrepresentation, Mistake and Non-Disclosure*, 5th edn (Sweet & Maxwell, 2019), para.4-77.

(f) Causation.

Replace n.109 with:

8-020   109 *UCB Corporate Services Ltd v Williams* [2002] EWCA Civ 555; [2003] 1 P. & C.R. 12. See too *Syndicate Bank v Dansingani* [2019] EWHC 3439 (Ch) at [96], where HHJ Dight rejected A's argument that B must show that, "had she been fully informed she would not have entered into the transaction", stating instead that: "If [B] did not enter into the transaction of her own free will she did not consent to it and she has a right in principle to set the transaction aside."

3. Applying the Test for Undue Influence

(c) "Presumed" undue influence: The special class of established relationships of influence.

Replace n.143 with:

[143] See, e.g. J. Edelman & E. Bant, *Unjust Enrichment in Australia* (OUP, 2006) 221; K. Lewison, "Under the Influence" [2011] *Restitution Law Review* 1, 9; C. Mitchell et al (eds), *Goff & Jones: The Law of Unjust Enrichment*, 9th edn (Sweet & Maxwell, 2016), paras 11–47.

8-024

(f) "Presumed" undue influence: Rebutting the presumption.

Replace n.234 with:

[234] This formulation was cited with approval in *Syndicate Bank v Dansingani* [2019] EWHC 3439 (Ch) at [97]. See *Etridge* [2002] 2 A.C. 773 HL at [111], per Lord Hobhouse: "It is their weakness which is being protected not their inability to comprehend".

8-033

4. Remedies

Replace first paragraph with:

It has been judicially stated that:

8-037

"[t]here is no 'obligation' not to exercise undue influence in order to persuade a party to enter into a contract. The party exercising undue influence incurs no liability. It is merely that the party whose consent was obtained by the exercise of undue influence is entitled to have the contract set aside."[250]

The primary remedy for undue influence is, therefore, rescission and so general rules applying to that form of relief, as set out in Ch.15, are of relevance.[251] For example, the standard equitable defences of laches, acquiescence and confirmation may prevent relief even if undue influence has been established.[252] B's failure to seek relief when remaining under the undue influence should not however be held against B, no matter how long the influence endures.[253] After the influence has ceased B must however commence the proceedings within a reasonable time[254] or the court may draw the inference that he or she has elected to affirm the transaction.[255]

[250] *Agnew v Lansforsakringsbolagens AB* [2001] 1 A.C. 223 HL at 265. Lord Millett's speech was in dissent, but no disagreement was expressed with his observation as to the nature of undue influence.

[251] See too paras 2-006—2-008 for discussion of the effect of a mere equity on a third party. In *Mortgage Express v Lambert* [2016] EWCA Civ 555, Lewison LJ confirmed at [16] that B's right to set aside a transfer of registered land on the grounds of undue influence (or on the grounds of an unconscionable bargain) is a "mere equity" and thus is capable of binding a successor in title to A: s.116(b) of the Land Registration Act 2002. On the facts of that case, however, any such right of B had been overreached as C's mortgage had been granted by two trustees: see [39]. See too *Davies v AIB Group (UK) Plc* [2012] EWHC 2178 (Ch) at [119] where Norris J stated that, had undue influence been found, B would in any case have been estopped from denying liability under the impugned loan contract because of B's acceptance of renewed and especially extended facilities (untainted by any undue influence) under the same loan contract. Note though that if a mortgage procured by undue influence is replaced with a substantially identical mortgage, B has a prima facie power to rescind that substitute mortgage, even if the undue influence did not persist at the time of B's entry into that later mortgage: *Yorkshire Bank Plc v Tinsley* [2004] EWCA Civ 816. See also, N. Gravells "Undue Influence and Substitute Mortgages" [2005] 64 C.L.J. 42.

[252] See, e.g. *Goldsworthy v Brickell* [1987] Ch. 378 at 410; *Elton John v James* [1991] F.S.R. 397. See too *de Sena v Notaro* [2020] EWHC 1031 (Ch) at [233].

[253] *Hatch v Hatch* (1804) 9 Ves. 292 (20 years). An attempt to raise laches was also rejected in *Curtis v Curtis* [2011] EWCA Civ 1602 at [20]–[24].

[254] See *Bullock v Lloyds Bank Ltd* [1955] Ch. 317 (4 years after influence had ceased and discovery of remedy). Compare *Humphreys v Humphreys* [2004] EWHC 2201 (Ch) at [103] (4 years' delay not sufficient to bar claim for undue influence). See also *Allcard v Skinner* (1887) 36 Ch. D. 145 (6 months after influence had ceased and discovery of remedy). But note the exceptional facts of *Allcard v Skinner* where C had had access to legal advice and the inference was drawn that she had made a conscious choice not to seek the return of the property.

[255] For examples of affirmation of transactions induced by undue influence see *Allcard v Skinner* (1887) 36 Ch. D. 145 and *Turner v Collins* (1871) 7 Ch. App. 329. Knowledge of the choice (which will include the legal right to set it aside) will normally be required before B can be held to have affirmed the transaction although if B deliberately declines to investigate circumstances which might give rise to a claim this may give rise to an inference of affirmation: see P Feltham et al (eds) Spencer Bower *Reliance-Based Estoppel* , 5th edn (Bloomsbury, 2017) at 13.26.

Replace second paragraph with:

8-039   It may seem that *Mahoney v Purnell*[268] provides some support for a jurisdiction to order A to pay compensation in an undue influence case: A no longer held the right transferred in the impugned transaction, nor did A retain the proceeds of sale or any other traceable proceeds of that right. May J nonetheless held that "[p]ractical justice in this case requires an award which is akin to damages"[269] and so A was ordered to pay B a sum to prevent B's suffering a loss as a result of A's inability to return the right transferred. The award was said to be based on A's "abuse of trust", however, and it can be readily be explained as a means of redressing A's clear breach of a fiduciary duty owed to B: as a result, it does not provide a general basis for relief premised on B's loss rather than on A's gain.[270]

[268] *Mahoney v Purnell* [1996] 3 All E.R. 61. Note too that in *Jennings v Cairns* [2003] EWCA Civ 1935, where the impugned transaction was a settlement on trusts to pay the school fees of A's children, A was personally ordered to return the value of the money settled, even though the relief sought did not include setting aside the settlement, and A had received the money, strictly, in her capacity as a trustee. The validity of such a personal order was not however challenged, either at first instance or in the Court of Appeal (see at [45] per Arden LJ) and so the question of law was not considered. The best interpretation may well be that the sums were, in substance, paid for A's benefit, and A had continued access to them, so no hardship was caused by the order that she should repay them.

[269] *Mahoney v Purnell* [1996] 3 All E.R. 61 at 88. In *de Sena v Notaro* [2020] EWHC 1031 (Ch) at [230], HHJ Paul Matthews considered that, if (as was not the case) undue influence had been established, then, as rescission restoring the parties to their previous positions would have been impossible, an enquiry would have been needed as to whether "some other remedy could be awarded, such as equitable compensation".

[270] See too C. Mitchell et al (eds) *Goff and Jones: The Law of Unjust Enrichment*, 9th edn (Sweet & Maxwell, 2016) 11–28.

4. UNCONSCIONABLE TRANSACTIONS

3. Application of the Test

(a) Vulnerability.

Replace n.290 with:

8-043   [290] See *Chagos Islanders v Attorney General* [2003] EWHC 2222 (QB) at [545]. In *Jones v Morgan* [2001] EWCA Civ 995 at [40] it was held that B (who was described as "naïve, trusting and unbusiness-like") was not acting under a relevant vulnerability because he had the benefit of legal advice: Chadwick LJ stated that "it is for a solicitor to advise the naïve, the trusting or the unbusiness-like in their dealings with the more astute. In such a case the client relies on the solicitor to protect his interests; and, if the solicitor is competent and fulfils his role, the imbalance which would otherwise exist by reason of the client's naiveté, trust and lack of business experience is redressed". In *de Sena v Notaro* [2020] EWHC 1031 (Ch) at [241], HHJ Paul Matthews, using the test for an unconscionable transaction set out at 8-042, found that B was not vulnerable as "she was an experienced business woman who dealt with business transactions day in, day out, as well as being a charity trustee."

(c) Knowing exploitation of vulnerability.

Replace n.295 with:

[295] *Boustany v Pigott* (1995) 69 P. & C.R. 298 PC at 303. See too *de Sena v Notaro* [2020] EWHC 1031 (Ch) at [241].   **8-045**

CHAPTER 9.

BREACH OF CONFIDENCE

1. Origins and Scope of the Jurisdiction

1. Origins

Replace n.1 with:

9-001

[1] For recent comprehensive examinations of the detail of the doctrine of breach of confidence, see C. Phipps et al (eds), *Toulson & Phipps on Confidentiality*, 4th edn (Sweet & Maxwell, 2020); and T. Aplin et al (eds) *Gurry on Breach of Confidence*, 2nd edn (OUP, 2012). P Stanley, *The Law of Confidentiality: A Restatement* (Hart, 2008) is shorter but is another useful specialist work.

Replace n.4 with:

[4] As noted in T. Aplin et al (eds) *Gurry on Breach of Confidence*, 2nd edn (2012), 2.87: "*Prince Albert v Strange* was not the first time the law had protected confidentiality – not by a long way". *Abernethy v Hutchison* (1825) 1 H. & Tw. 28, 47 E.R. 1313 is suggested as an earlier example of the recognition in equity of a non-contractual duty of confidence.

2. Scope

(a) No need for a contractual relationship or a proprietary right.

Replace n.9 with:

9-002

[9] A question which has been heavily debated in the cases and the academic literature but which may ultimately involve circular reasoning since it often depends upon what is meant by "property": see Phipps et al (eds), *Toulson & Phipps on Confidentiality*, 4th edn (2020) para.2–033; R. Dean, *The Law of Trade Secrets and Personal Secrets*, 3rd edn (Lawbook Co, 2018) at [2.140]–[2.150]. Compare *Boardman v Phipps* [1967] 2 A.C. 46 HL at 89–90, 102 and 127–128 (Lords Dilhorne, Cohen and Upjohn suggesting that information is not property) with 107 and 115 (Lords Hodson and Guest suggesting that it is).

(f) Impact of the Human Rights Act 1998.

Replace n.37 with:

9-008 [37] *Douglas v Hello! Ltd* [2008] 1 A.C. 1 at [255], per Lord Nicholls: "a trade secret may be protected as confidential information even though no question of personal privacy is involved". For consideration of when such commercial information may be confidential, see, e.g. *Faccenda Chicken Ltd v Fowler* [1987] Ch. 117 CA; *Lansing Linde Ltd v Kerr* [1991] 1 W.L.R. 251; as applied in, e.g. *Personal Management Solutions Ltd v Brakes Bros Ltd* [2014] EWHC 3495 (QB) at [191]–[196]; and *Marathon Asset Management LLP v Seddon* [2017] EWHC 300 (Comm); [2017] I.C.R. 791 at [115]–[117]. See too *Trailfinders Ltd v Travel Counsellors Ltd* [2020] EWHC 591 (IPEC), where HHJ Hacon at [27] drew on the definition of "trade secret" in Art.2(1) of the Trade Secrets Directive 2016/943, implemented by the Trade Secrets (Enforcement, etc) Regulations 2018, as providing "the best guide to the distinction between information which is confidential and that which is not".

(g) Future of the doctrine.

Replace n.41 with:

9-009 [41] For arguments to this effect see e.g. T. Aplin, "The Future of Breach of Confidence and the Protection of Privacy" (2007) 7 Oxford University Commonwealth Law Journal 137; C. Phipps et al (eds), *Toulson & Phipps on Confidentiality*, 4th edn (Sweet & Maxwell, 2020), ch.7.

(h) Nature of the cause of action: is breach of confidence a tort?

Replace n.54 with:

9-010 [54] M. Jones (eds), *Clerk and Lindsell on Tort*, 23rd edn (Sweet & Maxwell, 2020), Ch.26.

Replace n.61 with:

[61] In *Vidal-Hall v Google Inc* [2016] Q.B. 1003 CA, for example, the question was whether a breach of confidence/misuse of private information claim was a claim "made in tort" where damage had been sustained within the jurisdiction, so that service out of the jurisdiction was permitted by para.3.1(9) of Practice Direction 6B, supplementing Pt 6 of the Civil Procedure Rules. The Court of Appeal drew a distinction between the breach of confidence and misuse of private information claims, finding that the latter had no inherently equitable characteristics and that there was no good reason to regard the claim as not arising in tort, stating at [48] that: "It would seem an odd and adventitious result for the defendant, if the historical accident of the division between equity and the common law resulted in the claimants in the present case being unable to serve their claims out of the jurisdiction". That approach was approved in *Gulati v MGN Ltd* [2016] 2 W.L.R. 1217: see, per Arden LJ at [88]. Note too the distinction between confidence-focused and privacy-focused claims drawn by the Supreme Court in *PJS v News Group Newspapers Ltd* [2016] A.C. 1081 SC and Lord Mance's references at [32]–[33], [38] and [44] to the "tort of invasion of privacy", or to "tortious invasion of privacy". In *JQL v NTP* [2020] EWHC 1349 (QB), in the context of the publication of confidential and private information, HHJ Lewis at [133] referred to both breach of confidence and misuse of private information as torts. In *The Racing Partnership Ltd v SIS Ltd* [2020] EWCA Civ 1300, Arnold LJ at [70] stated that, following *Vidal-Hall v Google*, "breach of confidence and misuse of private information are two separate and distinct causes of action which rest on different legal foundations and protect different interests, and hence a claim for misuse of private information is 'made in tort' even though a claim for breach of confidence is an equitable one."

2. THE TEST AND ITS APPLICATION

(b) Reasonable expectation that the information is confidential or private.

Replace n.78 with:

9-013 [78] *James v James* (1872) 41 L.J. Ch. 353; *Reuters Telegram Co v Byron* (1874) 43 L.J. Ch. 661; *Saltman Engineering Co Ltd v Campbell Engineering Co Ltd* (1948) 65 R.P.C. 203 at 215; [1963] 3 All E.R. 413 at 415, per Lord Greene MR; *Seager v Copydex (No.1)* [1967] 1 W.L.R. 923 CA at 932, per Lord Denning MR; *Coco v A N Clark (Engineers) Ltd* [1969] R.P.C. 41 at 49, per Megarry J; *Woodward v Hutchins* [1977] 1 W.L.R. 760; *O Mustad & Son v Dosen (Note)* [1964] 1 W.L.R. 109. Note that information will not lose the quality of confidence simply because it is known to a small number of people: see, e.g. *AB v Sunday Newspapers (t/a The Sunday World)* [2014] NICA 58 at [26]; and *Warwickshire CC v Matalia* [2015] EWHC B4 (Ch) at [35] (affirmed on appeal: [2017] EWCA Civ 991). This is also the case where information is merely used by A, rather than being published by A: *Kerry Ingredients Ltd v Bakkavor Group Ltd* [2016] EWHC 2448 (Ch) at [62] (Newey J). Similarly, information is not rendered non-confidential simply because, with a significant amount of work, that information could be acquired through reverse engineering: ibid. at [67]. In *The Racing Partnership Ltd v SIS Ltd* [2020] EWCA Civ 1300, members of the Court of Appeal took different views as to whether particular racing information, in the very brief period before it became publicly available, could be regarded as confidential: see Arnold LJ at [65]-[77] and contrast with the view of Lewison LJ (with whom Philipps LJ agreed) at [179]-[189].

(c) Knowledge of the confidentiality of the information.

Replace n.92 with:

⁹² See, e.g. *Campbell v MGN Ltd* [2004] 2 A.C. 457 HL. Conversely, of course, if a reasonable person in A's position would not have regarded the information as confidential then no liability will arise, even if a more sophisticated legal analysis would have led to the conclusion that the information was confidential: as noted by Lewison LJ in *The Racing Partnership Ltd v SIS Ltd* [2020] EWCA Civ 1300 at [206], it would be wrong to attribute to A an inappropriate "degree of legal knowledge and analytical skills."

9-014

(d) Knowledge of confidentiality where C is a third party.

Replace n.105 with:

¹⁰⁵ Note too that C may also be liable on the basis of a common design if C shares "with the other party, or parties, to the design, each of the features of the design that make it wrongful":*Vestergaard Frandsen A/S v Bestnet Europe Ltd* [2013] UKSC 31; [2013] 1 W.L.R. 1556 at [34], per Lord Neuberger. Where C is A's employer, it seems that C may also be vicariously liable, in a suitable case, for a breach of confidence committed by A in the course of A's employment: see, e.g. *Vestergaard Frandsen A/S v Bestnet Europe Ltd* [2013] UKSC 31; [2013] 1 W.L.R. 1556 at [34], per Lord Neuberger at [27]; *Primary Group (UK) Ltd v Royal Bank of Scotland* [2014] EWHC 1082 (Ch) at [249] per Arnold J. See too *Axon v Ministry of Defence* [2016] EWHC 787 (QB) at [95], where it was found that, had A's employee committed the "tort" of misusing private information, then it would have been a suitable case to find her employer vicariously liable. In *Various Claimants v WM Morrison Supermarkets Plc* [2018] EWCA Civ 2339; [2019] Q.B. 772 it was held that a claim based on an employer's vicarious liability for breach of confidence or misuse of personal information was not expressly or impliedly excluded by the operation of the Data Protection Act 1998 ([148]–[162]). On appeal, the Supreme Court ([2020] UKSC 12) reversed the finding that vicarious liability arose on the facts of the case, but agreed (at [54]-[55]) that the 1998 Act did not exclude liability for misuse of private information and breach of confidence.

9-015

3. REMEDIES

2. Damages and Equitable Compensation

Replace second paragraph with:

Whether B seeks damages on the basis of the statutory power, the equitable jurisdiction, or (in an appropriate case) on A's breach of a contractual duty of confidence, the assessment of damages proceeds in the same way¹⁵⁷: the court calculates the damages based on the sum which would put B in the same position as if the breach of confidence had not occurred.¹⁵⁸ These damages can include consequential losses for distress and disappointment.¹⁵⁹ Although, in line with tort claims, awards for distress and disappointment should be modest,¹⁶⁰ where the distress and exposure of the victim is widespread and significant the damages awarded can be as much as £60,000.¹⁶¹

9-020

¹⁵⁷ *Johnson v Agnew* [1980] A.C. 367 HL at 400–401, per Lord Wilberforce demonstrates that the assessment under the statute is governed by the same rules applying in the general law.

¹⁵⁸ *Indata Equipment Supplies Ltd v ACL Ltd* [1998] B.C.L.C. 412; C. Phipps et al (eds), *Toulson & Phipps on Confidentiality*, 4th edn (Sweet & Maxwell 2020) 6–164. In *Force India Formula One Team Ltd v 1 Malaysia Racing Team* [2012] EWHC 616 (Ch) at [407] Arnold J cast doubt on the Court of Appeal's willingness in *Indata* to draw an analogy with the tort measure, but it would be a mistake, it is submitted, to view that measure, in this context, as distinct from a "contract measure": whatever the source of A's duty, the central aim of damages is to put B in the position B would have been in had the duty been performed and this means, for example, that relief can be awarded in relation to financial loss,

including lost profits, suffered by B as a result of A's breach: see, e.g. *Flogas Britain Ltd v Calor Gas Ltd* [2013] EWHC 3060 (Ch); [2014] F.S.R. 34 at [37]–[41], per Proudman J.

[159] *Campbell v MGN Ltd* [2004] 2 A.C. 457 HL; *Douglas v Hello! Ltd (No.8)* [2004] E.M.L.R. 2; [2006] Q.B. 125 CA. Aggravated damages may also be awarded: see e.g. *JQL v NTP* [2020] EWHC 1349 (QB) [160]-[164]. Consistently with the approach of the Supreme Court in *R. (on the application of Lumba) v Sec of State for the Home Dept* [2012] 1 A.C. 245, damages for breach of confidence or misuse of private information are "not the same as vindicatory damages to vindicate some constitutional right", but can compensate for loss of the right to control the use of private information: see e.g. *Gulati v MGN Ltd* [2016] 2 W.L.R. 1217 at [45]-[49]. Arden LJ also noted there that damages can thus "compensate (if appropriate) for the loss of privacy or autonomy as such arising out of the infringement" (ibid at [168]).

[160] In *Douglas v Hello! Ltd (No.6)* [2006] Q.B. 125, the Court of Appeal upheld an award to each of B1 and B2, of which £3,750 was compensation for the distress caused by the publication of the unauthorised photographs, with a further £7,000 for the cost and inconvenience for having to make a hurried selection of authorised photographs when the magazine to which they had given exclusive rights brought publication forward to compete with A.

[161] *Mosley v News Group Newspapers Ltd* [2008] EWHC 1777; [2008] E.M.L.R. 20. Eady J noted there at [216] that the "scale of the distress and indignity in this case is difficult to comprehend. It is probably unprecedented". See too *Cooper v Turrell* [2011] EWHC 3269 (QB), where A's deliberate dissemination of a falsehood was also a relevant factor in assessing damages and a figure of £40,000 would have been awarded to B if the sole claim had been for breach of confidence. The discussion in this paragraph was referred to by Tugendhat J at [94]. In *Gulati v MGN Ltd* [2016] 2 W.L.R. 1217, the Court of Appeal upheld sizable damages awards for misuse of the private information of victims of phone-hacking, with the highest individual award (based on 31 separate publications) being £260,250.

5. Exemplary Damages

Replace second paragraph with:

9-024   It was worth noting that, whilst Eady J refused to characterise breach of confidence as a "tort",[202] he did not suggest that exemplary damages should be denied merely because of the jurisdictional origin of breach of confidence in the Court of Chancery.[203] As noted above,[204] such questions should instead be determined by the particular nature of the claim made, as well as, of course, the general arguments for and against exemplary damages.[205] It has been observed that any award of exemplary damages for a breach of confidence might constitute a disproportionate interference with A's art.10 right to freedom of expression,[206] although it should not be assumed that art.10 is always engaged where breach of confidence is concerned,[207] and it can also be noted that exemplary damages are in principle available in defamation.[208] Lord Nicholls stated that "the availability of exemplary damages should be co-extensive with its rationale … the underlying rationale lies in the sense of outrage which a defendant's conduct sometimes evokes, a sense not always assuaged by a compensatory award of damages, even when the damages are increased to reflect emotional distress".[209] On this view, it is not difficult to think of particular breaches of confidence that might give rise to that sense of outrage.[210]

[202] *Mosley v News Group Newspapers Ltd* [2008] EWHC 1777; [2008] E.M.L.R. 20 at [184] and [190]. Contrast, e.g. *Vidal-Hall v Google Inc* [2016] Q.B. 1003; and *PJS v News Group Newspapers Ltd* [2016] A.C. 1081, where misuse of confidential information has been regarded as, and referred to, as a tort: see fn.37.

[203] Contrast the view taken by Heydon JA in *Harris v Digital Pulse Ltd* [2003] NSWCA 10; (2003) 56 N.S.W.L.R. 298; and criticised by, e.g. A. Burrows, "Remedial Coherence and Punitive Damages in Equity" in S. Degeling & J. Edelman (eds), *Equity in Commercial Law* (Thomson, 2006).

[204] See para 9-010.

[205] For arguments against, see, e.g. Lord Scott in *Kuddus v Chief Constable of Leicestershire* [2002] 2 A.C. 122 at [95]-[111]. For arguments in favour, see, e.g. J. Edelman "In Defence of Exemplary Damages" in C. Rickett (ed), *Justifying Private Law Remedies* (Hart, 2003), 225.

[206] *Mosley v News Group Newspapers Ltd* [2008] EWHC 1777; [2008] E.M.L.R. 20 at [193]. Note too Human Rights Act 1998 s.12(1).

[207] As noted at para.9-018, A's misuse of confidential information need not involve any communication of that information.

[208] See, e.g. *Broome v Cassell & Co Ltd* [1971] 2 Q.B. 354 CA.

[209] *Kuddus v Chief Constable of Leicestershire* [2002] 2 A.C. 122 HL at [65].

[210] See too C. Phipps et al (eds), *Toulson & Phipps on Confidentiality*, 4th edn (Sweet & Maxwell, 2020) 6-187. Note that in *Mosley v News Group Newspapers Ltd* [2008] EWHC 1777; [2008] E.M.L.R. 20, Eady J at [180] rejected a contention, based on Lord Nicholls' "general observations" in *Kuddus*, that "all that is required [for exemplary damages] is conduct characterized as 'outrageous'", and refused to award exemplary damages even whilst noting at [216] that the "scale of the distress and indignity in this case is difficult to comprehend. It is probably unprecedented".

CHAPTER 10.

POWERS—GENERAL PRINCIPLES

5. CONTROLLING POWERS

After "first place. The", add:

10-017   first consequence of this difficulty is that the courts are cautious about interfering in the purported exercise of a power: the power holder should be allowed to act unless a good reason can be shown to justify the court's intervention.[41a] The second consequence is that the constraints on the exercise of a power are

[41a] *Lehtimaki v Cooper* [2020] UKSC 33.

1.   Controls on Powers Which Concern the Scope of a Power

(b)   Good Faith

Replace seventh paragraph with:

10-019   Both good faith and bad faith are ascertained prima facie by reference to actual, subjective, states of mind. This has often been emphasised in judicial decisions, whether they concern trustees,[66] or directors.[67] However, the holder of a fiduciary power who exercises it in a self-interested way will not be taken to be acting in good faith.[68] Furthermore, a fiduciary power exercised for reasons of caprice or spite will not be exercised in good faith.[69]

[66] See, e.g. *Re Smith* [1896] 1 Ch.71 at 76, per Kekewich J (in relation to powers of investment); *Bristol & West Building Society v Mothew* [1998] Ch. 1 at 18; and *Armitage v Nurse* [1998] Ch. 241 at 253–254, per Millett LJ (general principle); *Lehtimaki v Cooper* [2020] UKSC 33 at [100], [187], per Lady Arden. However, the position appears to be different in Australia, where "good faith" is used to encompass matters other than a subjective state of mind: see, e.g. *Re Marsella; Marsella v Wareham (No 2)* [2019] VSC 65 at [36], per McMillan J.

[67] *Re Smith & Fawcett Ltd* [1942] Ch. 304 at 306; *Medforth v Blake* [2000] Ch. 86 at 103, per Scott VC; *Regentcrest Plc (In Liquidation) v Cohen* [2001] 2 B.C.L.C. 80 (ChD) at [120], per Jonathan Parker J. See also *Extrasure Travel Insurances Ltd v Scattergood* [2002] EWHC 3093 (Ch); [2003] 1 B.C.L.C. 598 at [87]–[90], per Jonathan Crow QC.

[68] *Howard Smith Ltd v Ampol Petroleum Ltd* [1974] A.C. 821 at 834, per Lord Wilberforce; citing *Fraser v Whalley* 2 Hem. & M. 10; and *Hogg v Cramphorn Ltd* [1967] Ch. 254.

[69] *Re Smith* at 76; *Bristol & West Building Society v Mothew* [1998] Ch. 1 at 18; *Armitage v Nurse* [1998] Ch. 241 at 253.

After the seventh paragraph, add new paragraph:

In very unusual circumstances, where a court has approved a course of action as being in the interests which the fiduciary must further, it would be a breach of the fiduciary's duty of good faith to do anything other than implement that course of action.[69a] As Lord Briggs put it in the context of a charitable trust:

> "[O]nce the court's decision about the merits of the transaction is made then, subject to any appeal (or perhaps a significant change in circumstances before it is implemented), that difficult question has been finally resolved. It ceases to be a question for debate. It is binding on all those interested parties joined to the relevant proceedings, and the duty of the charity's fiduciaries (whether or not joined as parties) is to use their powers to the end that it is implemented, both generally and in accordance with any directions which the court may give for that purpose. It would in my view be a plain breach of fiduciary duty for a relevant fiduciary of the charity to do otherwise, a fortiori to exercise a fiduciary power so as in effect to veto the very transaction which the court has decided should proceed in furtherance of the charity's purposes."[69b]

By contrast, good faith action can even include unauthorised action in some cases.[70]

[69a] *Lehtimaki v Cooper* [2020] UKSC 33 at [205]-[235], per Lord Briggs, with whom Lords Wilson and Kitchin agreed.

[69b] *Lehtimaki v Cooper* [2020] UKSC 33 at [208]. See also at [218].

[70] *Armitage v Nurse* [1998] Ch. 241 at 251, 253–254, per Millett LJ.

(c)   Fraud on a Power/Improper Purposes

Replace seventh paragraph with:

High authority also confirms that the doctrine of abusing a power for an improper **10-020** purpose is not the same as simply exceeding the power: the proper purposes doctrine and questions of construction are distinct in how they seek to control discretionary power. Lord Wilberforce noted the distinction in *Howard Smith v Ampol Petroleum*:

> "The directors, in deciding to issue shares, forming part of Millers' unissued capital, to Howard Smith, acted under clause 8 of the company's articles of association. This provides, subject to certain qualifications which have not been invoked, that the shares shall be under the control of the directors, who may allot or otherwise dispose of the same to such persons on such terms and conditions and either at a premium or otherwise and at such time as the directors may think fit. Thus, and this is not disputed, the issue was clearly intra vires the directors. But, intra vires though the issue may have been, the directors' power under this article is a fiduciary power: *and it remains the case that an exercise of such a power though formally valid, may be attacked on the ground that it was not exercised for the purpose for which it was granted.*"[85]

Lord Sumption put the matter as follows in *Eclairs Group v JKX Oil & Gas Plc*

> "… the proper purpose rule is not concerned with excess of power by doing an act which is beyond the scope of the instrument creating it as a matter of construction or implication. It is concerned with abuse of power, by doing acts which are within its scope but done for an ulterior purpose."[85a]

[85] *Howard Smith v Ampol Petroleum* [1974] A.C. 821 at 834, emphasis added. See also *Fearon v Desbrisay* (1851) 14 Beav. 635 at 642; 51 E.R. 428 at 431, per Romilly MR; and *Henty v Wrey* (1882) 21 Ch. D. 332 at 355, per Lindley LJ.

[85a] [2015] UKSC 71; [2016] 1 B.C.L.C. 1 at [15].

Ascertaining what amounts to a fraud on a power.

Replace fourth paragraph with:

The exercise of ascertaining a settlor's expectations may be more or less **10-022** evidentially difficult. When making its findings, the court may or may not have the assistance of a letter of wishes,[94] or other admissible evidence. Clarke P of the Court of Appeal for Bermuda put it as follows in *Grand View Private Trust Co Ltd v Wong*:

> "[I]t seems to me that, when considering the equitable rule that a power may not be used otherwise than in accordance with the purpose for which it was given (even if the use falls within the scope of the terms of the trust) Equity should not, in a case such as this, close her mind to extrinsic evidence of the settlor's intentions, when setting up the trust and when granting the power, particularly when it is the wishes of the settlor that the trustee is required to take into account when deciding on the exercise of the power. To do so would not offend the rules of construction or implication because the evidence would only be relevant after it had been concluded that the proposed exercise of the power was not outlawed as a matter of construction or implication."[94a]

[94] See *Re Rabiotti's 1989 Settlement* [2000] W.T.L.R. 953 at 967–968, per Deputy Bailiff Birt (Jersey Royal Court, Samedi Division); *Breakspear v Ackland* [2008] EWHC 220 (Ch); [2009] Ch. 32 at [5]–[14], and esp. at [8], per Briggs J, though "[i]t may be that there are some matters in the memorandum

[of wishes] which…it would not be proper for the trustees to take into account in the exercise of any, or of a particular, discretionary power": *Hartigan Nominees Pty Ltd v Rydge* (1992) 29 N.S.W.L.R. 405 at 427, per Mahoney JA. See also *Grand View Private Trust Co Ltd v Wong* [2020] CA (Bda) 6 Civ.

[94a] [2020] CA (Bda) 6 Civ at [218].

After the fourth paragraph, add new paragraph:

A court may encounter evidential difficulties in some cases, for example where a trust has more than one settlor, or where a trust has been amended,[95] varied under the Variation of Trusts Act 1958, or created out of another settlement.[96] The terms of a trust (or other organisation) may have evolved over time; and in such a case, the observations of Millett J in *In re Courage Group's Pension Schemes Ryan v Imperial Brewing and Leisure* will be relevant:

> "[I]n the case of an institution of long duration and gradually changing membership like a club or pension scheme, each alteration in the rules must be tested by reference to the situation at the time of the proposed alteration, and not by reference to the original rules at its inception. By changes made gradually over a long period, alterations may be made which would not be acceptable if introduced all at once. Even the main purpose may be changed by degrees…"[96a]

If the court does encounter such problems, then it can supply default implications, if needs be fashioned by reference to "reasonable expectations". This might seem a similar exercise to the control of power in public law by reference to Wednesbury unreasonableness.[97] Nevertheless, the court should be very cautious about any such analogy between private and public law. In the private law context, the court is primarily engaged in a forensic exercise to establish a purpose, or purposes, and should only make implications in so far as it is defeated in that exercise. The court is not, as in public law, applying mandatory rules of law (or at least very strong default presumptions) generated by policy concerns of constitutional legitimacy and propriety.[98] As Lord Sumption put it in *Eclairs Group v JKX Oil & Gas Plc*:

> "Ascertaining the purpose of a power where the instrument is silent depends on an inference from the mischief of the provision conferring it, which is itself deduced from its express terms, from an analysis of their effect, and from the court's understanding of the business context."[98a]

[95] A power to amend trusts is common in pension trusts: see R. Self, *Pension Fund Trustee Handbook*, 9th edn (Haywards Heath: Tottel Publishing, 2005) at para.6.3, and, by way of example, *Imperial Group Pension Trust Ltd v Imperial Tobacco Plc* [1991] 1 W.L.R. 589.

[96] See, generally, A.J. Oakley, *Parker and Mellows: The Modern Law of Trusts*, 9th edn (London: Sweet & Maxwell, 2008) at [18–024]–[18–044]; and Lord Millett, *Encyclopedia of Forms and Precedents*, 5th edn (London: Butterworths, 2001), Vol.40(1) at paras 139 (settled advances); and 4359 and 4405 (powers for trustees to appoint trust funds to distinct settlements).

[96a] [1987] 1 W.L.R. 495, 506, cited with approval by Lord Walker in *Bank of New Zealand v Board of Management of the Bank of New Zealand Officers Provident Association* [2003] UKPC 58 at [19].

[97] *Scott v National Trust* [1998] 2 All E.R. 705 at 718g. The charity involved in this case, the National Trust for Places of Historic Interest or Natural Beauty, is actually a corporation rather than a trust stricto sensu: see the National Trust Act 1907 s.3. That should not affect this point, however.

[98] See *Underhill & Hayton: Law of Trusts and Trustees* (2006), paras 61.12–61.17. Rather ironically, the continuing place of *Wednesbury* unreasonableness in administrative law is moot: see, generally, H.W.R. Wade & C.F. Forsyth, *Administrative Law*, 9th edn (Oxford: Oxford University Press, 2004) at 371–372.

[98a] [2015] UKSC 71; [2016] 1 B.C.L.C. 1 at [30].

CHAPTER 12.

ESTOPPEL

1. INTRODUCTION

2. Estoppel at Common Law

Estoppel by representation.

Replace n.14 with:

[14] See, e.g. *Burkinshaw v Nicolls* (1878) 3 App. Cas. 1004; *Re Concessions Trust* [1896] 2 Ch. 757; and see *Robinson v Montgomeryshire Brewery Co* [1896] 2 Ch. 841. There is a substantial case law dealing with estoppels arising out of the transfer of shares: see P. Feltham et al (eds), *Spencer Bower's Reliance-Based Estoppel*, 5th edn (Bloomsbury, 2017), paras 10.19-10.21.   **12-005**

3. Estoppel in Equity

(c) Estoppel by convention.

Replace n.38 with:

[38] Adopted by Carnwath LJ in *ING Bank NV v Ros Roca SA* [2011] EWCA Civ 353; [2012] 1 W.L.R. 472 at [55]–[60] and described there as "a succinct statement of the modern law, adopted without dissent or qualification by the full House of Lords", the formulation was also accepted by the parties and court in *Robert Sofer v Swissindependent Trustees SA* [2020] EWCA Civ 699 at [53]. For a helpful summary of the "principles applicable to the assertion of an estoppel by convention arising out of non-contractual dealings", see *HMRC v Benchdollar Ltd* [2009] EWHC 1310 (Ch), per Briggs J at [52]; and note too *Mears Ltd v Shoreline Housing Partnership Ltd* [2015] EWHC 1396 (TCC), per Akenhead J at [51].   **12-011**

Replace para.12-012 with:

12-012   The doctrine may therefore apply where the party against whom the estoppel by convention is raised made no representation or promise. It nonetheless resembles estoppel by representation in its effect (it determines the facts on which the parties' rights are to be determined, rather than itself providing a cause of action).[41] As a result of the decision of the Court of Appeal in *Amalgamated Investment & Property Co Ltd v Texas Commerce International Bank Ltd*,[42] estoppel by convention is now more often regarded as a variant of equitable estoppel[43] and seen as defining a particular set of circumstances in which it is "unjust",[44] or unconscionable,[45] to allow a party to go back on an underlying assumption that formed the basis of a transaction.

[41] See G. Treitel, *Some Landmarks of Twentieth Century Contract Law* (Oxford: OUP, 2002), 38–41, distinguishing between estoppels which relate to facts (such as estoppel by representation or estoppel by convention) and those which instead relate to legal effects (such as promissory estoppel and proprietary estoppel). In *Mears Ltd v Shoreline Housing Partnership Ltd* [2015] EWHC 1396 (TCC), Akenhead J at [71] noted that: "Although there are distinguishing features between the two types of estoppel [by representation and by convention], there must be cases, and this is one, where the two are almost interchangeable on the facts".

[42] *Amalgamated Investment & Property Co Ltd v Texas Commerce International Bank Ltd* [1982] Q.B. 84.

[43] See, e.g. *PW & Co v Milton Gate Investments Ltd* [2004] Ch. 142 at [156], and at [238]; *ING Bank NV v Ros Roca SA* [2011] EWCA Civ 353; [2012] 1 W.L.R. 472 at [73], per Carnwath LJ.

[44] In addition to the statement of Lord Steyn set out at para.12-011, see too *Amalgamated Investment & Property Co Ltd v Texas Commerce International Bank Ltd* [1982] Q.B. 84 at 122, per Lord Denning MR.

[45] *Norwegian American Cruises A/S v Paul Mundy Ltd ("The Vistafjord")* [1988] 2 Lloyds Rep. 343 at 352; *Gloyne v Richardson* [2001] 2 B.C.L.C. 669 CA at 683–684; *PW & Co v Milton Gate Investments Ltd* [2004] Ch. 142 at [156], [165], [209], and [221]. In *Blindley Health Investments Ltd v Bass* [2015] EWCA Civ 1023, Hildyard LJ noted at [72] that estoppel by convention was originally developed by the common law courts, but that "especially since the decision of this court in *Amalgamated Investment & Property Co Ltd (in liquidation) v Texas Commerce International Bank Ltd* [1982] 1 Q.B. 84, its principles have largely been explained in equitable terms and expanded as another variant of equitable estoppel" and at [73] referred with approval to this paragraph.

Replace n.56 with:

12-014   [56] *Grundt v Great Boulder Proprietary Gold Mines Ltd* (1937) 59 C.L.R. 641 at 676, per Dixon J. Dixon J's analysis on this point was approved by the Privy Council in *Prime Sight Ltd v Lavarello* [2013] UKPC 22; [2014] A.C. 436 at [23] and [46] per Lord Toulson: the general position is that "parties to a transaction may choose to enter into it on the basis that certain facts are to be treated as correct as between themselves for the purposes of the transaction, although both know that they are contrary to the true state of affairs, in which case the necessary convention for an estoppel will be established". See too *ING Bank NV v Ros Roca SA* [2011] EWCA Civ 353; [2012] 1 W.L.R. 472 at [85], where an estoppel by convention arose even though, as Rix LJ noted at [85], one of the parties did not internally share the assumption, but affected and purported to share it externally and objectively. If however a party makes a representation knowing it to be false, and the other party believes it to be true, then it is at least arguable that there is no shared assumption such as to support an estoppel by convention: see *Robert Sofer v Swissindependent Trustees SA* [2020] EWCA Civ 699 at [56].

2.   PROMISSORY ESTOPPEL

2.   The Requirements of Promissory Estoppel

(c)   Legal relationship.

Replace n.171 with:

12-026   [171] In an obiter discussion in *Harvey v Dunbar Assets Plc* [2017] EWCA Civ 60 at [62], Henderson LJ noted the view expressed here, and, whilst preferring to express no concluded view on the question, stated that: "it seems clear to me that the weight of existing authority supports the view that promissory estoppel can only arise in the context of an existing legal relationship, as Lord Walker said in *Thorner v Major*". It was therefore doubted that promissory estoppel could apply as a result of a promise (that a guarantee would not be enforced) made to induce B to provide the guarantee to A. In any case, on the facts, it was implausible for B, an experienced business person, to expect that A would under no circumstances enforce the guarantee. Henderson LJ stated at [65] that "It is simply not credible that [B] proceeded to execute the Guarantee on the footing that he was engaging in a solemn farce, and that it would never in any circumstances be enforced against him". In *Umrish Ltd v Gill* [2020] EWHC 1513 (Ch), it was similarly found by Simon Salzedo QC, sitting as a Deputy Judge, that no promissory estoppel could arise from an alleged pre-contractual promise of A not to enforce a guarantee entered into with B, where the reliance would consist of entry into the "very legal relationship which the promise is said to have varied. There is an inherent contradiction between the promise not to enforce certain terms and the act done in supposed reliance upon it, viz. agreement to those very terms." It was also stated at [101] that: "It seems to me, in respectful agreement with Henderson LJ in *Harvey v Dunbar Assets*, that authority in England and Wales is strongly to the effect that promissory estoppel requires the pre-existence of a legal relationship between the promisor and promisee." The nature of the alleged promise meant that, "[e]ven if the law might develop further in terms of broader equitable restraints on conduct, it does not cover a case like this one" (at [102]).

(d)   Reliance by B.

Replace n.184 with:

[184] *Steria Ltd v Hutchison* [2006] EWCA Civ 1551; [2007] I.C.R. 445 at [128]–[129]. Neuberger LJ's **12-027** approach was applied in *Univar UK Ltd v Smith* [2020] EWHC 1596 (Ch) at [359]-[360].

3.   PROPRIETARY ESTOPPEL

1.   Nature and Origins of the Modern Doctrine

(a)   General formulation.

Replace para.12-033 with:

In *Thorner v Major*,[235] Lord Walker noted the scholarly consensus that **12-033** proprietary estoppel:

> "is based on three main elements ... a representation or assurance made to the claimant; reliance on it by the claimant; and detriment to the claimant in consequence of his (reasonable) reliance."

In line with this approach, which regards proprietary estoppel as a unitary doctrine, the law will be examined below by reference to the requirements of the general formulation set out above. It is important to note, however, that this general formulation cannot be, nor was intended to serve as, a test that can be applied, without more, to determine the practical operation of proprietary estoppel to a particular set of facts.[236] Rather, it is submitted, a distinction must be made between the three distinct strands that comprise the current law of proprietary estoppel[237]: after all, as noted by Lord Walker,[238] "synthesis and unification, however desirable as objectives, have their dangers".

[235] *Thorner v Major* [2009] UKHL 18; [2009] 1 W.L.R. 776 at [29].

[236] See, e.g. *Macdonald v Frost* [2009] EWHC 2276 (Ch); [2010] 1 P. & C.R.D.G. 14 at [9], per Geraldine Andrews QC, where the three part test is prefaced by the observation that: "there is still no comprehensive and uncontroversial definition of proprietary estoppel".

[237] The distinction between the acquiescence, representation and promise-based strands of proprietary estoppel is made by J. Mee, "Proprietary Estoppel, Promises and Mistaken Belief" in S. Bright (ed.), *Modern Studies in Property Law* (Oxford: Hart Publishing, 2011), Vol.6, pp.175, 181–183; and by B. McFarlane, "Understanding Equitable Estoppel: From Metaphors to Better Laws" (2013) *Current Legal Problems* 1. It is developed in B. McFarlane, *The Law of Proprietary Estoppel* 2nd edn (Oxford: Oxford University Press, 2020). K. Low, "Nonfeasance in Equity" (2012) 128 L.Q.R. 63 at 72–73 and I. Samet, "Proprietary Estoppel and Responsibility for Omissions" (2015) 78 M.L.R. 85, also identify the point

that the law of proprietary estoppel may be based on distinct principles which require distinct justifications. In *Hoyl Group Ltd v Cromer Town Council* [2015] EWCA Civ 782, Floyd LJ stated at [72] that: "A proprietary estoppel does not have to fit neatly into the pure acquiescence-based pigeon hole or the assurance one" and also endorsed the broad approach to proprietary estoppel adopted by Oliver J in *Taylors Fashions Ltd v Liverpool Victoria Trustees Co Ltd* [1982] Q.B. 133 at 151–152; but this may simply reflect that, in the *Hoyl Group* case, the relevant conduct of A consisted both of failing to provide information to B and requesting that B complete particular work. In *Mohammed v Gomez* [2019] UKPC 46, the Board doubted at [26] "how far it is possible or useful in the context of proprietary estoppel to draw fine distinctions between different categories", but this may similarly reflect the factual context, as A's failure to object to B's building on A's land was seen by the court below as supporting both the finding of an agreement and a distinct acquiescence-based claim.

[238] *Cobbe v Yeomans Row Management Ltd* [2008] UKHL 55; [2008] 1 W.L.R. 1752 at [48].

(b) An acquiescence-based principle.

Replace n.244 with:

12-034 [244] This formulation of acquiescence based estoppel was relied on by Judge Simon Baker QC in *Mills v Partridge* [2020] EWHC 2171 (Ch) at [121]. It was suggested in the previous edition (at para.12-016) that the acquiescence principle responds to A's unjust enrichment at B's expense. That suggestion is considered further by K. Low, "Nonfeasance in Equity" (2012) 128 L.Q.R. 63. As noted at fn.239, the principle instead has been said to be based on the need to prevent dishonest or fraudulent conduct by A: see e.g. *Willmott v Barber* (1880) 15 Ch. D. 96, per Fry J at 105; *Electrolux Ltd v Electrix Ltd* (1954) 71 R.P.C. 23 CA, per Sir Raymond Evershed MR at 33; *Shaw v Applegate* [1977] 1 W.L.R. 970 CA, per Buckley LJ at 978. For discussion of the possible moral bases of the principle, see I. Samet, "Proprietary Estoppel and Responsibility for Omissions" (2015) 78 M.L.R. 85.

(c) A representation-based principle.

Replace n.255 with:

12-035 [255] In *Hopgood v Brown* [1955] 1 W.L.R. 213 CA, the estoppel also bound the claimant in the case, a successor in title to A and this seems to be one respect in which the general rules of estoppel by representation may seem to operate differently in the proprietary context, even if it consists only of extending the scope of the estoppel's preclusive effect, rather than the generation of a cause of action. For full discussion of the rule surrounding the effect of an estoppel by representation on a third party, see e.g. B. McFarlane, *The Law of Proprietary Estoppel*, 2nd edn (2020), 8.47–8.64. Note that a different view is taken in P. Feltham et al (eds) *Spencer Bower's Reliance-Based Estoppel*, 5th edn (Bloomsbury, 2017) where it is argued at 12.3 that an estoppel by representation can give rise to an equitable cause of action where it relates to rights over or in property.

2. The Requirements of Proprietary Estoppel

(a) Representation or assurance made to B.

Replace n.308 with:

12-039 [308] For instructive cases in which the required promise was absent see, e.g. *Cook v Thomas* [2010] EWCA Civ 227; and *Lissimore v Downing* [2003] 2 F.L.R. 308. For further discussion of the principles and factors relevant to the finding of a promise see B. McFarlane, *The Law of Proprietary Estoppel*, 2nd Edn (2020), 2.213–2.249.

Replace first paragraph with:

12-040 It is certainly the case that a proprietary estoppel cannot arise where B simply hopes to acquire a right in A's land, and so does not have any belief that he has, or will necessarily acquire, such a right.[310] The submission as to the need for a promise must, nonetheless, be made with some caution, as it is a simple matter to find formulations of the test for proprietary estoppel that refer only to the need for A to have "encouraged" B's belief as to A's future conduct.[311] Indeed, in *Hoyl Group Ltd v Cromer Town Council*, the Court of Appeal adopted "encouragement" as the relevant test, thereby seemingly rejecting counsel's submission that a promise is required where B acts on the basis of a belief as to acquiring rights in the future.[312] On the facts of the case, however, the success of the estoppel claim in *Hoyl Group* is not, it is submitted, inconsistent with the need for a promise[313] and the idea that encouragement alone suffices in a case where B relies on a belief as to acquiring rights in the future is, it is submitted, inconsistent with the result in *Cobbe* and the reasoning of the House of Lords in *Thorner*.[314]

[310] See, e.g. *Cobbe v Yeoman's Row Management Ltd* [2008] UKHL 55; [2008] 1 W.L.R. 1752, per Lord Walker at [64]: "It is not enough to hope, or even to have a confident expectation, that the person who has given assurances will eventually do the right thing". See also *Hoyl Group Ltd v Cromer Town Council* [2015] EWCA Civ 782, per Floyd LJ at [61]: "I accept that it is necessary for [B] to show that they believed that they had or would have a right of way via the garden access". See too *Curran v Collins* [2015] EWCA Civ 404 [69], where Lewison LJ noted that: "it cannot be right that the giving of a reason why someone is not on the title deeds inevitably leads to the inference that it must have been agreed that they would have an interest in the property." If such an excuse is however linked to a "positive representation" that the house would otherwise have been put in joint names (as in *Eves v Eves* [1975] 1 W.L.R. 1338 (CA) and *Grant v Edwards* [1986] Ch 638 (CA)) then it may be possible to infer the required assurance: see Lewison LJ ibid at [69]-[74].

[311] See, e.g. *Taylors Fashions Ltd v Liverpool Victoria Trustees Co Ltd* [1982] Q.B. 133 (Ch) at 145, 151–152; *Re Basham* [1986] 1 W.L.R. 1498 at 1503. Note that cases analysed here as applying the promise-based principle are sometimes said to be part of a doctrine of "estoppel by encouragement" (rather than of "estoppel by standing by"): see, e.g. *Joyce v Epsom and Ewell BC* [2012] EWCA Civ 1398 at [39]; *Hoyl Group Ltd v Cromer Town Council* [2015] EWCA Civ 782 at [65]–[75]; K. Handley, *Estoppel by Conduct and Election* (London: Sweet & Maxwell, 2006), pp.163–165; *Sullivan v Sullivan* [2006] NSWCA 312 at [4].

[312] *Hoyl Group Ltd v Cromer Town Council* [2015] EWCA Civ 782 at [65]–[75] (Floyd LJ). In *Smyth-Tyrrell v Bowden* [2018] EWHC 106 (Ch), having considered *Hoyl*, HHJ Paul Matthews QC at [77] considered that it "seems correct in principle" that a claim can be based on B's reliance on a belief that A will in the future give B a right, even in the absence of a promise by A, if A either knows of B's belief and does nothing to disabuse it or, even if A does not know of B's belief, A "nonetheless positively encourages [B] to act in ways only consistent with [B's] having such a belief (so that, objectively speaking, it should be obvious to [A] what is going on)". See too the view of the same judge in *Gilpin v Legg* [2017] EWHC 3220 (Ch) at [102].

[313] In *Hoyl Group*, it seems first that B was found by the trial judge to have relied on a belief as to its current rights ([2015] EWCA Civ 782 at [63]) and secondly that the facts (like those of *Thorner v Major* [2009] UKHL 18; [2009] 1 W.L.R. 1776) would have supported the finding of an implied promise.

[314] In *Inwards v Baker* [1965] 2 Q.B. 29 CA, the Court of Appeal held expressly that a promise was not required for B to succeed. In that case, however, in contrast to the claimants in *Thorner* and *Cobbe*, B was not seeking to establish a cause of action, but instead wished simply to resist an application for possession made by the trustees of A's will. It may therefore be possible to explain the result in the case by reference to different principles, which do not require a promise to be made, such as waiver (see para.12-021). In *Crabb v Arun DC* [1976] Ch. 179 CA at 188, Lord Denning MR stated explicitly that a cause of action based on proprietary estoppel could arise in cases where A's conduct was "[s]hort of an actual promise", relying on a statement of Cotton LJ in *Birmingham & District Land Co v London & North Western Railway Co (No.2)* (1888) 40 Ch. D. 268 CA at 277. As discussed at para.12-020, however, the principle applied in the *Birmingham* case cannot operate as a cause of action. It is significant that, in *Cobbe* [2008] UKHL 55; [2008] 1 W.L.R. 1752, Lord Walker (at [79]) described *Crabb* as a "difficult case": it is submitted that the difficulty lies in finding any express or implied promise by A. For support for the contrary view that encouragement short of a promise suffices for a proprietary estoppel claim, even where B's belief relates to A's future conduct, see A Robertson, "The Form and Substance of Equitable Estoppel" in A Robertson & J Goudkamp (eds) *Form and Substance in the Law of Obligations* (Hart, 2019).

(b) Reliance by B.

Replace fourth paragraph with:

The position in the promise-based strand is less than clear. Certainly, A's promise **12-043** need not provide the sole reason for B's action: it is very rarely the case that B will act for just one reason and, for example, a claim may still arise even where B cares for A not only as a result of a testamentary promise but also because of the ties of family or friendship.[343] Beyond this, however, it is often merely stated that there must be a "sufficient causal link between the assurance relied upon and the detriment asserted".[344] An argument can be made that the standard "but for" test should apply.[345] Certainly, if A can show that B would have acted in the same way, and so still be facing the same risk of detriment, even in the absence of A's promise, it is difficult to see why A should now bear responsibility for that risk of detriment. In *Wayling v Jones*,[346] a rather odd test was adopted, as the court considered not what B would have done in the absence of A's promise, but rather what B would have done had A informed B that A was not going to honour the promise. Such a test is very favourable to B, and is hard to justify, as the relevant conduct of A on which B's claim is based is the promise, not A's failure to tell B that it will not be honoured.[347] It has also been stated that, whilst A's promise does not have to be the sole inducement for B's conduct, it is sufficient if it is an inducement.[348] Support for a test asking if A's promise was a contributing factor to B's conduct can also be found in *van Dyke v Sidhu*, where four of the judges of the High Court of Australia applied a test which asked if "the promises in question contributed to [B's] conduct"[349] and based their finding of reliance on the fact that A's promises had been found by the primary judge to have "played a part" in B's decision to act.[350] Nonetheless, in almost all of the cases in which B's claim has succeeded,[351] the finding of reliance has been, on the facts, compatible with a test asking if, but for A's promise, B would still have adopted the course of conduct now claimed to give rise to the risk of detriment. For example, in *van Dyke v Sidhu*, the fifth judge, Gageler J adopted, in effect, a "but for" test and found that it too had been met on the facts.[352]

[343] See, e.g. *Campbell v Griffin* [2001] EWCA Civ 990 at [29], per Robert Walker LJ.

[344] See, e.g. *Gillett v Holt* [2001] Ch. 210 CA at 232, per Robert Walker LJ; *Wayling v Jones* (1993) 60 P. & C.R. 170 at 173, per Balcombe LJ.

[345] For a full survey of the different possibilities, and an argument in favour of the standard "but for" test: see B. McFarlane, *The Law of Proprietary Estoppel*, 2nd edn (2020), 3.114–3.212.

[346] *Wayling v Jones* (1993) 69 P. & C.R. 170 CA.

[347] For academic criticism of the *Wayling* test, see, e.g. E. Cooke, "Reliance and Estoppel" (1995) 111 L.Q.R. 389 and *The Modern Law of Estoppel* (Oxford: OUP, 2000) 111; J. Mee, *The Property Rights of Co-Habitees* (Oxford: Hart, 1999) 108; B. McFarlane, *The Law of Proprietary Estoppel*, 2nd edn (2020), 3.114–3.132.

[348] See, e.g. *Campbell v Griffin* [2001] EWCA Civ 990 at [29], per Robert Walker LJ; *Century (UK) Ltd SA v Clibbery* [2004] EWHC 1870 (Ch) at [73], per Blackburne J.

[349] *Van Dyke v Sidhu* [2014] HCA 19 at [66], per French CJ, Kiefel, Bell and Keane JJ.

[350] *Van Dyke v Sidhu* [2014] HCA 19 at [71], per French CJ, Kiefel, Bell and Keane JJ.

[351] *Ottey v Grundy* [2003] EWCA Civ 1176; [2003] W.T.L.R. 1253 may be an exception: see B. McFarlane, *The Law of Proprietary Estoppel*, 2nd edn (2020), 3.125-3.129.

[352] *Van Dyke v Sidhu* [2014] HCA 19 at [93], per Gageler J: the test as stated there asks what B would have done in the absence of the assumption (that B would acquire a right in A's land), but in a promise case, it is more accurate, it is submitted, to ask what B would have done in the absence of A's promise. If B would have had the same belief without A's promise then no claim should arise. Compare *Western Fish Products Ltd v Penwith District Council* [1981] 2 All E.R. 204 CA: no estoppel arose where, independently of any representation by A, B had in any case an "absolute conviction" of the truth of the fact on which it relied.

Replace n.354 with:

12-043 [354] *Van Dyke v Sidhu* [2014] HCA 19 at [57]. See too B. McFarlane, *The Law of Proprietary Estoppel*, 2nd edn (2020) 3.233–3.256, also pointing out that Lord Denning had applied principles developed in the context of fraudulent misrepresentations to the quite different context of the promise-based strand of proprietary estoppel.

(d) The role of unconscionability.

Replace n.381 with:

12-045 [381] *Cobbe v Yeoman's Row Management Ltd* [2008] UKHL 55; [2008] 1 W.L.R. 1752 at [92] per Lord Walker. For the additional use of this concept of unconscionability in aiding a court to interpret the three main elements of proprietary estoppel, see B. McFarlane, *The Law of Proprietary Estoppel*, 2nd Edn (2020), Ch.5.

Replace n.382 with:

382 See, e.g. *Guest v Guest* [2020] EWCA Civ 387 at [59]-[61] and [79] at [276]. In *Habberfield v Habberfield* [2019] EWCA Civ 890, it was argued by A that B's earlier refusal to accept an offer to run A's farm in partnership with A meant that it was not unconscionable for A later to fail to keep an assurance that B would take over the running of the farm on A's retirement and then inherit the farm, or at least that any reliance by B after that point should be discounted. That argument was rejected on the basis that the partnership offer did not fulfil the assurance that B would be able to run the farm (see [30]) and that A had not made an "unambiguous final offer" that if rejected would then prevent B from continuing to rely on past assurances by A (at [44]).

(e) Formality requirements and other possible bars.

Replace n.390 with:

390 See, e.g. *Chalmers v Pardoe* [1963] 1 W.L.R. 677 PC (distinguished in *Maharaj v Chand* [1986] A.C. **12-046** 898 PC); and in *Brightlingsea Haven Ltd v Morris* [2008] EWHC 1928 (QB); [2009] 2 P. & C.R. 11 at [60]: for discussion see B. McFarlane, *The Law of Proprietary Estoppel*, 2nd Edn (2020) 6.136–6.141); *ER Ives (Investments) Ltd v High* (1967) 2 Q.B. 379 at 395 (relief would have been refused if it had involved an infringement of s.13 of the Land Charges Act 1925); *Mayor and Burgesses of the London Borough of Bexley v Maison Maurice Ltd* [2006] EWHC 3192 (Ch) at [56] (relief would not have been granted if it would have involved ordering A to act beyond its legal powers).

Replace n.400 with:

400 The analysis in this paragraph was referred to by Falk J in *Sahota v Prior* [2019] EWHC 1418 (Ch) at [34] as supportive of the conclusion there reached that s.2 did not prevent B's proprietary estoppel claim where A had made assurances as to B's right to remain in occupation of property transferred by B under a sale and leaseback arrangement. It was also favoured by Judge Mark Raeside QC in *Wills v Sowray* [2020] EWHC 939 (Ch) at [259]-[262]. The analysis finds further support in the (obiter) discussion of the point by Kitchin LJ (with whom Floyd and Patten LJJ agreed) in *Farrar v Miller* [2018] EWCA Civ 172 at [57]-[63]. See further B. McFarlane, "Proprietary Estoppel and Failed Contractual Negotiations" [2005] Conv. 501. Versions of this basic view are also are also supported by M. Dixon, "Confining and Defining Proprietary Estoppel" (2010) 30 L.S. 408; and G. Owen & O. Rees, "Section 2(5) of the Law of Property (Miscellaneous Provisions) Act 1989: A Misconceived Approach" [2011] Conv. 495. See too the very useful discussion of the point by Master Matthews in *Muhammad v ARY Properties Ltd* [2016] EWHC 1698 (Ch) at [32]-[51], respectfully expressing the view at [49] that the exception created by s.2(5) for constructive trusts "appears to be a red herring, because proprietary estoppel is not about enforcing a contract at all". For recent academic discussion of the point see T. Boncey and F. Ng, "'Common Intention' Constructive Trusts Arising from Informal Agreements to Dispose of Land" [2017] Conv. 146 and M. Dixon, "More Moves in Constructive Trusts and Estoppel" [2017] Conv. 89.

3. Relief

(a) Overview.

Replace n.410 with:

410 See *Davies v Davies* [2016] EWCA Civ 463; [2016] 2 P. & C.R. 10 at [39], where Lewison LJ notes **12-047** (without on the facts of the case needing to resolve) the "lively controversy" on the issue. In *Guest v Guest* [2020] EWCA Civ 387 at [48], Floyd LJ stated that the courts have avoided such controversy by simply finding "a remedy that is appropriate in all the circumstances of the case to satisfy the equity that has arisen, and so to avoid an unconscionable result." That analysis risks, however, overlooking the usual distinction (made by Scarman LJ in *Crabb v Arun DC* [1976] Ch 9 (CA), 198) between first establishing the extent of B's equity and then determining the best remedy, in practice, to give effect to the equity; indeed Floyd LJ at [72] doubted the usefulness of that distinction, stating that a court could instead ask "a single question: what is necessary to avoid an unconscionable result?" For academic discussion see, e.g. S. Gardner "The Remedial Discretion in Proprietary Estoppel" (1999) 115 L.Q.R. 438; and "The Remedial Discretion in Proprietary Estoppel – Again" (2006) 122 L.Q.R. 492; S. Bright and B. McFarlane, "Proprietary Estoppel and Property Rights" [2005] C.L.J 449; J. Mee, "Expectation and Proprietary Estoppel Remedies" in M. Dixon (ed.) *Modern Studies in Property Law* (Vol.5) 389; A Robertson, "The Reliance Basis of Proprietary Estoppel Remedies" [2008] Conv. 295; Y Liew, "The 'Prima Facie Expectation Relief' Approach in the Australian Law of Proprietary Estoppel" (2019) 39 O.J.L.S. 183. See too B. McFarlane, *The Law of Proprietary Estoppel*, 2nd Edn (2020) Ch.7.

(c) Two competing approaches.

Replace para.12-049 with:

12-049   Beyond this common ground, however, uncertainty arises as the courts have yet to choose clearly between two competing approaches.[424] On the first approach, the starting point is that B's expectation will be protected, and a departure from this is permitted only if it is clear that such an order would impose a disproportionate burden on A. On this view, then, the concept of proportionality[425] has only a negative role to play.[426] On the second approach, there is no presumption in favour of making B's expectation good, and the extent of relief will be determined principally by the need for such relief to do no more than ensuring that B suffers no detriment as a result of B's reasonable reliance on A[427]; although B may be left to suffer some detriment if A can show that such an outcome would not, on the facts, "shock the conscience of the court".[428] The first approach has gained some recent support in Australia[429] and in the Court of Appeal.[430] It is submitted, however, that the better approach is the second. It is supported by the reasoning in a number of Court of Appeal[431] and Privy Council[432] cases.[433] A logical difficulty with the first approach is that it allows for the possibility that, in two cases where the extent of B's prospective detriment is identical, the value of B's right may increase as a result of the value of B's expectation decreasing.[434] It may well also be the case that the first approach is based on the assumption that proprietary estoppel is an adaptation of estoppel and so A should, generally, be precluded from denying B's expectation. The difficulty with this view, however, is that, when proprietary estoppel is applied to acquiescence promises, rather than to representations, it escapes the reach of such preclusive logic.[435] The second approach, as it gives a positive role to the need for proportionality, and defines the concept by reference to the extent of B's potential detriment, also improves on the first by providing principles that can be used to determine the extent of B's right even when it is clear that B's expectation should not be protected.[436] It also draws an important link between the grounds on which B's right arises (the need to avoid B's being left to suffer a detriment) and the extent of that right. As noted by Lewison LJ in *Davies v Davies*: "Since the essence of proprietary estoppel is the combination of expectation and detriment, if either is absent the claim must fail. If, therefore, the detriment can be fairly quantified and a claimant receives full compensation for that detriment, that compensation ought, in principle, to remove the foundation of the claim".[437] With one exception,[438] it is also difficult to find decisions where the result reached is inconsistent with the second approach.[439]

---

[424] See *Davies v Davies* [2016] EWCA Civ 463; [2016] 2 P. & C.R. 10 at [39], where Lewison LJ stated that: "There is a lively controversy about the essential aim of the exercise of this broad judgmental discretion. One line of authority takes the view that the essential aim of the discretion is to give effect to the claimant's expectation unless it would be disproportionate to do so. The other takes the view that the essential aim of the discretion is to ensure that the claimant's reliance interest is protected, so that she is compensated for such detriment as she has suffered". At one point, it would have been possible to say that English courts favoured the first, more traditional view, and Australian courts the second (see, e.g. the judgments of Mason CJ, Brennan and McHugh JJ and Toohey J in *Commonwealth of Australia v Verwayen* (1990) 170 C.L.R. 394). More recently, it has been possible to say the opposite (compare, e.g. *Sledmore v Dalby* [1996] 72 P. & C.R. 196 CA and *Henry v Henry* [2010] UKPC 3; [2010] 1 All E.R. 988 with, e.g. *Giumelli v Giumelli* (1999) 196 C.L.R. 101, noted by J. Edelman "Remedial Certainty or Remedial Discretion in Estoppel after Giumelli?" (1999) 7 *Journal Contract Law* 179, and the cases noted in fn.411). For further analysis of the Australian case law, see Y. Liew, "The 'Prima Facie Expectation Relief' Approach in the Australian Law of Proprietary Estoppel" (2019) 39 O.J.L.S. 183. In *Low Heng Leon Andy v Low Kian Beng Lawrence* [2018] S.G.C.A. 48, Andrew Phang J argued that the dichotomy between the two approaches is a false one, as both expectation and detriment must be accounted for and the method adopted by the court will depend on how B chooses to plead the case: for

discussion and criticism see Y Liew, *"The Remedial Approach to Proprietary Estoppel in Singapore"* [2020] Conv 11.

[425] The concept of proportionality is itself a source of some uncertainty, as it has not always been clearly defined. In *Jennings v Rice* [2002] EWCA Civ 159; [2003] 1 P. & C.R. 8, for example, Aldous LJ, at 36 emphasised the need for "proportionality between the expectation and the detriment". This may be read to mean that the extent of B's right must be proportionate to both the expectation and detriment (the interpretation given by, e.g. S. Gardner "The Remedial Discretion in Proprietary Estoppel – Again" (2006) 122 L.Q.R. 492, at 498) but, as it is very difficult to see how proportionality to two different measures can be maintained, it seems more likely that, as Aldous LJ was responding to an argument that B's right should be set by B's expectation, the statement means that B's expectation will be protected only if that would be proportionate to the extent of B's detriment (this interpretation is preferred by, e.g. J. Mee, "Expectation and Proprietary Estoppel Remedies" in M. Dixon (ed.) *Modern Studies in Property Law* (Vol.5) pp.389, 404 fn.59).

[426] This view has been favoured in, e.g. *Suggitt v Suggitt* [2012] EWCA Civ 1140; [2012] W.T.L.R. 1607 at [44]–[45], per Arden LJ; *James v James* [2018] EWHC 43 (Ch) at [51]–[52] and [62] and *Brake v Swift* [2020] EWHC 1810 at [151], per HHJ Paul Matthews; and, in Australia, in e.g. *Delaforce v Simpson-Cook* (2010) 78 N.S.W.L.R. 483; and *Harrison v Harrison* [2013] V.S.C.A. 170.

[427] This view can be supported by e.g. *Sledmore v Dalby* (1996) 72 P. & C.R. 196 CA at 208, per Hobhouse LJ (quoting from Mason CJ in *Commonwealth of Australia v Verwayen* (1990) 170 C.L.R. 394, at 413): "A central element of the doctrine is that there must be a proportionality between the remedy and the detriment which is its purpose to avoid"; and *Henry v Henry* [2010] UKPC 3; [2010] 1 All E.R. 988 at [65], per Sir Jonathan Parker: "Proportionality lies at the heart of the doctrine of proprietary estoppel and permeates its every application"; see too *Arif v Anwar* [2015] EWHC 124 (Fam) at [96], where Norris J asked: "what relief is right and conscionable to grant so as to ensure that [B] suffers no detriment".

[428] This seems to follow from Lord Walker's general statement of principle in *Cobbe v Yeoman's Row Management Ltd* [2008] UKHL 55; [2008] 1 W.L.R. 1752 at [92]. As noted at para.12-045, the concept of unconscionability may be invoked in a promise-based case where a significant change of circumstances means that the burden of performance is now much greater than anticipated: in some cases, such a change might not remove A's liability entirely, but rather reduce it, as implied by Mummery LJ in *Uglow v Uglow* [2004] EWCA Civ 987 at [30].

[429] See, e.g. *Giumelli v Giumelli* (1996) 196 C.L.R. 101; *Delaforce v Simpson-Cook* (2010) 78 N.S.W.L.R. 483; and *Harrison v Harrison* [2013] VSCA 170.

[430] *Suggitt v Suggitt* [2012] EWCA Civ 1140; [2012] W.T.L.R. 1607 at [44]–[45], per Arden LJ. In *Guest v Guest* [2020] EWCA Civ 387 at [48], Floyd LJ, referring to the two different approaches identified in *Davies v Davies* as to the aim of the remedial discretion, stated that "the courts have shown a marked reluctance to answer a question posed in such stark terms. The courts have preferred to identify its aim or task as the fashioning of a remedy that is appropriate in all the circumstances of the case to satisfy the equity that has arisen, and so to avoid an unconscionable result." It was found that, on the facts of the case, "the overall outcome came close to the expected reciprocal performance of the acts requested in return for the assurance. The judge was therefore entitled to take [B's] expectation as a strong factor in deciding how to satisfy the equity." This result is consistent with either of the two approaches: see 12.050.

[431] See *Davies v Davies* [2016] EWCA Civ 463; [2016] 2 P. & C.R. 10 at [39], where Lewison LJ, without having to decide on the facts between the two different approaches set out above, stated that "Logically, there is much to be said for the second approach". See too *Habberfield v Habberfield* [2019] EWCA Civ 890 at [57], where Lewison LJ disagreed with the statement of Arden LJ in *Suggitt v Suggitt* [2012] EWCA Civ 1140 at [44] that there does not need to be a relationship of proportionality between the level of detriment and the relief awarded. In *Moore v Moore* [2018] EWCA Civ 2669, Henderson LJ stated at [89] and [95] that the first instance judge had erred by making an order trying to mirror B's expectation rather than focussing on "the minimum provision that was needed to satisfy [B's] equity". See too *Dodsworth v Dodsworth* (1973) 228 E.G. 115 CA; *Crabb v Arun District Council* [1976] Ch. 179 at 198, per Scarman LJ (referring to the "minimum equity to do justice"); *Sledmore v Dalby* (1996) 72 P. & C.R. 196 CA at 208, per Hobhouse LJ; *Campbell v Griffin* [2001] EWCA Civ 990; *Jennings v Rice* [2002] EWCA Civ 159; [2003] 1 P. & C.R. 8; *Beale v Harvey* [2003] EWCA Civ 1883; [2004] 2 P. & C.R. 18 at [39], per Peter Gibson LJ; *Powell v Benney* [2007] EWCA Civ 1283.

[432] See *Clarke v Swaby* [2007] UKPC 1 at [18]; *Henry v Henry* [2010] UKPC 3; [2010] 1 All E.R. 988 at [65].

[433] See too, in Australia, *Commonwealth of Australia v Verwayen* (1990) 170 C.L.R. 394 (per Mason CJ, Brennan, McHugh and Toohey JJ); *Sullivan v Sullivan* [2006] NSWCA 312. Note also *Strover v Strover* [2005] EWHC 860 (Ch), treated it seems as an acquiescence case, where B's detriment consisted of losing the chance to propose to his fellow partners a variation in the terms of mirror life insurance policies, and B was awarded 80 per cent of the benefits that would have accrued from that change, to reflect the 20 per cent chance that the other partners might not have consented.

[434] This point is made by J. Mee, "Expectation and Proprietary Estoppel Remedies" in M. Dixon (ed.), *Modern Studies in Property Law: Volume V* (2009), pp.389, 399–400. For example, in *Jennings v Rice* [2002] EWCA Civ 159; [2003] 1 P. & C.R. 8, it was held that it would be disproportionate for B to receive A's house and furniture, valued at £435,000, and B was instead awarded £200,000. What if the house and furniture had instead been worth £250,000? It might well be said then that it would not be out of all proportion to order that the house and furniture be conveyed to B. If so, the extent of B's right would increase as a result of the decrease in value of A's property.

[435] See para.12-006.

[436] In *Moore v Moore* [2018] EWCA Civ 2669, Henderson LJ at [26] stated an initial view that "although the second approach is logically attractive, I would be wary of according it primacy in a field where cases are so fact sensitive and proportionality has such a prominent role to play". The point may simply be that, as will be seen in para.12-050, the second approach should not be applied in such a way as to mean that simply compensating B for quantifiable reliance loss will always be an appropriate way to satisfy an estoppel equity.

[437] See *Davies v Davies* [2016] EWCA Civ 463; [2016] 2 P. & C.R. 10 at [39], referring to A. Robertson, "The Reliance Basis of Proprietary Estoppel Remedies" [2008] Conv. 295.

[438] In *Pascoe v Turner* [1979] 1 W.L.R. 431 CA, A was ordered to transfer A's fee simple to B, where B's reliance on A's promise consisted of expending a relatively small sum on the property. The domestic context was important, and the need to ensure a "clean break" between the parties, so that A could not assert further pressure on B, was highlighted, but it would seem that, even adopting the first approach, the enforcement of B's expectation could be said to be "out of all proportion" to the detriment suffered.

[439] The reasoning in *Suggitt v Suggitt* [2012] EWCA Civ 1140; [2012] W.T.L.R. 1607 (e.g. at [44]–[45]) is certainly consistent only with the first view, but the result in the case may be seen as consistent with the second view once account is taken of the judge's (perhaps, on the facts, exaggerated) finding that B had "positioned his whole life on the basis of the assurances given to him". That finding was certainly important in the Court of Appeal's decision: see, e.g. at [23], [37], and at [38].

(d) Application of the suggested approach.

Replace n.446 with:

12-050 [446] *Habberfield v Habberfield* [2019] EWCA Civ 890 at [68]. See too *Guest v Guest* [2020] EWCA Civ 387 at [86].

Replace second paragraph with:

Even in such cases, however, "the expectation is not determinative of the relief to be granted".[447] In *Habberfield* itself, for example, whilst B had completed her side of a non-contractual quid pro quo, the Court of Appeal confirmed that the first instance judge had been correct to "scale down" the remedy awarded as a result of a change in the circumstances of A.[448] This demonstrates the underlying aim of the court's intervention, which is to ensure that A does not unconscionably leave B to suffer a detriment as a result of B's reliance on A's assurance.[449] The impact of taxation, where relevant, should also be taken into account in framing relief,[450] and in a case, for example, involving a claim for the transfer of valuable assets, the impact of inheritance tax, capital gains tax and income tax will require "careful consideration, with the benefit of expert evidence, or at least submissions from counsel well versed in the relevant areas of tax law".[451]

[447] *Habberfield v Habberfield* [2019] EWCA Civ 890 at [71] (Lewison LJ). See too *Moore v Moore* [2018] EWCA Civ 2669 at [30] where Henderson LJ noted that the factors set out by Robert Walker LJ in *Jennings* [2003] 1 P. & C.R. 8 at [52] (such as the need for a clean break and alternations in A's circumstances) are still relevant when considering a quasi-bargain case, although they are likely to have a less significant influence in such cases. For a reciprocal performance case where the need for a clean break was taken into account in determining relief, see e.g *Guest v Guest* [2020] EWCA Civ 387 at [89]; for one where alterations in A's circumstances were relevant, see *Habberfield v Habberfield* [2019] EWCA Civ 890 at [41].

[448] *Habberfield v Habberfield* [2019] EWCA Civ 890 at [41], [72]. B, a dairy farmer, had expected to acquire a working dairy farm but A had discontinued the dairy unit, and it was not suggested that A had acted culpably in so doing. As a result, the absence of the dairy unit was seen at [41] as "simply a change of circumstance which makes it inappropriate to give full effect to [B's] expectation" as the cost of reinstating the unit was estimated at £400,000. See too *Moore v Moore* [2018] EWCA Civ 2669 at [94],

where Henderson LJ pointed out that, even though B had spent his adult life working on A's farm in reliance on promises of inheritance on the death of the survivor of A and A's wife, with proper provision made for A's wife in the meantime, various changes of circumstance (e.g. the worsening health of A and the breakdown of relations in the family) meant that "this was no longer a realistic scenario".

[449] See further B McFarlane, *The Law of Proprietary Estoppel*, 2nd Edn (2020) 7.60–7.66. The possibility of taking into account circumstances arising after the time of B's reliance is also accepted by Hoffmann LJ's analysis in *Walton v Walton* (CA, 14 April 1994): see para.12-042.

[450] See *Jennings v Rice* [2002] EWCA Civ 159; [2003] 1 P. & C.R. 8 at [52], per Robert Walker LJ; *Habberfield v Habberfield* [2019] EWCA Civ 890 at [20], noting that the first instance judge had ordered A to pay a sum of money to B representing the value of A's farmland, and not to transfer the land itself, as a transfer of the farmland without the farmhouse would be "very tax inefficient" as the farmhouse would not then benefit from agricultural property relief from inheritance tax. See too *Guest v Guest* [2020] EWCA Civ 387 at [88], where the Court of Appeal approved of award framed with the aim, in part, of "mitigating the tax consequences" to A.

[451] *Moore v Moore* [2018] EWCA Civ 2669 at [96] (Henderson LJ). In that case, the first instance judge had made an order for the immediate transfer of assets worth around £5 million from A to B and that order, if implemented, would give rise to "significant CGT and income tax liabilities". Up to date valuations of the relevant assets are also required to allow the tax consequences of a contemplated order to be established. As Henderson LJ noted at [100], if a court does not have such information it may be necessary for a further hearing before the extent of the remedy can be determined.

Replace n.457 with:

[457] It is not always clear when a benefit will be seen as sufficiently related to B's acts of reliance as to have a countervailing effect: for an examination of the area, see B. McFarlane, *The Law of Proprietary Estoppel*, 2nd Edn (2020) 4.113–4.184.

Change title of sub-section:

4.   Effect on Third Parties.[472]

[472] The discussion here is focused on the possible imposition of the burden of a proprietary estoppel on a third party. A question may also arise as to the transfer of the benefit of a right arising through proprietary estoppel. In *Joyce v Epsom and Ewell Borough Council* [2012] EWCA Civ 1398, it was conceded that the benefit of an estoppel arising as a result of reliance on an expected easement did pass with the planned dominant tenement (noted J. Mee, "An Easement by Estoppel" [2013] Conv. 157, at 160–161). It has also been held that, on B's bankruptcy, the benefit of a proprietary estoppel claim will pass to B's trustee in bankruptcy: see *Webster v Ashcroft* [2011] EWHC 3848 (Ch); [2012] 1 W.L.R. 1309; and *Walden v Atkins* [2013] EWHC 1387 (Ch). For further discussion see B. McFarlane, *The Law of Proprietary Estoppel*, 2nd Edn (2020) at 8.160–8.182.

12-052

(c)   Position before a court order in B's favour.

Replace n.496 with:

[496] As noted by e.g. Lord Wilberforce in *National Provincial Bank v Ainsworth* [1965] A.C. 1175 at 1253, "[t]he fact that a contractual right can be specifically performed, or its breach prevented by injunction, does not mean that the right is any the less of a personal character or that a purchaser with notice is bound by it: what is relevant is the nature of the right, not the remedy which exists for its enforcement". The approach taken in this paragraph was discussed in *Brake v Swift* [2020] EWHC 1810 where the question was whether a proprietary estoppel equity arising as a result of B's reliance on a belief of acquiring a beneficial interest in land amounted to an "interest" in a dwelling-house under the revesting provisions of s.283A of the Insolvency Act 1986. HHJ Paul Matthews stated at [156]-[157] that it was not necessary on the facts to "give any view, much less a concluded view, about the scope of s.116 of the Land Registration Act 2002. It is sufficient for me to say that, in my judgment, the only proprietary estoppel claims which can properly be regarded as 'property' rights under the general law, binding third parties in the appropriate circumstances, are those of claims to already recognized property rights or interests."

12-054

CHAPTER 13.

PENALTIES AND FORFEITURE

1. OVERVIEW

(d) The relationship between the two doctrines.

Replace n.28 with:

[28] Lords Neuberger and Sumption in their joint judgment in *Cavendish* [2015] UKSC 67; [2016] A.C. **13-004**
1172 at [17]–[18]. The Supreme Court's decision in *Vauxhall Motors Ltd v Manchester Ship Canal Co Ltd* [2019] UKSC 46 did not consider in detail the relationship between penalties and forfeiture (although see Lady Arden at [72]–[73]). Note that the issue in that case was seen as one of relief against forfeiture whereas in *Vivienne Westwood Ltd v Conduit Street Development Ltd* [2017] EWHC 350 (Ch) the case was dealt with under the rule against penalties: in each case, B's breach of an agreement for the use of A's land led to A's attempting to exercise a contractual power to prevent B continuing to use that land under the existing terms, favourable to B. For academic consideration of the relationship between penalties and forfeiture in light of the Supreme Court's decision in *Vauxhall Motors*, see N Tiverios & B McFarlane, 'Controlling Private Punishment in Three Dimensions: Penalties and Forfeiture in England and Australia' in E Bant et al (eds) *Punishment and Private Law* (Hart, 2021).

2. PENALTIES

2. Scope of the Rule

(b) The need for a breach of contract.

Replace n.84 with:

[84] It may be that the somewhat unclear concept of a "disguised penalty", discussed at para.13-011, can **13-010**
provide some means of dealing with this paradox. For example, in *European Film Bonds AS v Lotus Holdings LLC* [2020] EWHC 1115 (Ch), the relevant term was contained in a guarantee agreement, so that B, the guarantor, suffered consequences as a result of a breach of contract committed by a different party. It was held that the clause was in any case not penal, so discussion of the point was obiter,

but the judge (Andrew Hochhauser QC) noted at [162]-[163] the submission that "the fact that the consequences of the breach are imposed on a different (non-breaching) party cannot be sufficient to turn a provision that is exorbitant or unconscionable into one which is not" as this would allow parties to circumvent the rule against penalties: "the substance of the contractual arrangements must be and are more important than the mere form."

3.   The Test for a Penalty

(a)   Summary of the test.

Replace n.119 with:

13-014   [119] *Talal El Makdessi v Cavendish Square Holding BV* [2015] UKSC 67; [2016] A.C. 1172 at [32]. Once it is determined that a clause is subject to review as a penalty, a materially identical test of whether the term is out of proportion to the legitimate interests of the innocent party in performance has been applied by the Supreme Court of New Zealand (*127 Hobson Street Ltd v Honey Bees Preschool Ltd* [2020] NZSC 53 at [56]-[57]) and by the High Court of Australia (*Paciocco v Australia and New Zealand Banking Group Ltd* [2016] HCA 28, (2016) 258 C.L.R. 525).

(c)   The concept of a "legitimate interest in performance".

Replace n.171 with:

13-018   [171] See, e.g. *Jeancharm Ltd v Barnet Football Club* [2003] EWCA Civ 58 at 20 per Keene LJ: "It is quite clear from the authorities that the concept of a penalty clause is not confined to situations where one party had a dominant bargaining power over the other, although it may, of course, often apply in such a situation". See too *Cavendish* [2015] UKSC 67; [2016] A.C. 1172 at [34] (Lord Neuberger and Lord Sumption); *127 Hobson Street Ltd v Honey Bees Preschool Ltd* [2020] NZSC 53 at [88].

(d)   An obligation which is exorbitant, unconscionable, or out of all proportion.

Replace n.176 with:

13-019   [176] *Cavendish* [2015] UKSC 67; [2016] A.C. 1172 at [75]. See too e.g. *European Film Bonds AS v Lotus Holdings LLC* [2020] EWHC 1115 (Ch) at [167]. In *127 Hobson Street Ltd v Honey Bees Preschool Ltd* [2020] NZSC 53 at [80]-[90], the fact that the term had been agreed between two commercial parties, and neither had taken advantage of the other, was relevant to a finding that the remedy it imposed was not out of all proportion to A's legitimate interest in performance. It was noted, for example, that agreeing to the term provided B with a way of making the "watertight commitment" ([16]) A was seeking as a condition of entering the contract.

(e)   Construction and timing.

Replace n.184 with:

13-020   [184] See, e.g *Triple Point Technology Inc v PTT Public Co Ltd* [2019] EWCA Civ 230 at [71] (an appeal to the Supreme Court is currently pending: the Court of Appeal decision is discussed by E Peel (2019) 135 L.Q.R. 530); *Dunlop Pneumatic Tyre Co v New Garage and Motor Co* [1915] A.C. 79 HL at 86, per Lord Dunedin: "Though the parties to a contract who use the words 'penalty' or 'liquidated damages' may prima facie be supposed to mean what they say, yet the expression used is not conclusive. The Court must find out whether the payment stipulated is in truth a penalty or liquidated damages". See e.g. *Alder v Moore* [1961] 2 Q.B. 57 CA; and *Robert Stewart & Sons Ltd v Carapanayoti & Co Ltd* [1962] 1 W.L.R. 34: the use of the term "penalty" to describe a clause was not decisive as the clause in each case was held in fact to be a genuine pre-estimate of damage and so enforceable in full.

4.   Remedial Issues

(a)   The effect of finding that a term is penal.

After "As noted at", replace "para.13-XXX," with:

13-023   para.13-004,

3.   RELIEF AGAINST FORFEITURE

2.   Scope of the Jurisdiction

(b)   Protecting a proprietary or possessory right.

Replace n.252 with:

[252] *Vauxhall Motors Ltd v Manchester Ship Canal Co Ltd* [2019] UKSC 46 at [49]–[51], affirming **13-028** [2019] Ch. 331 CA. In the Court of Appeal Lewison LJ noted at [52]–[53] that, to the extent that Australian law might suggest that the equitable jurisdiction can apply to contractual licences (see Edelman J in *Mineralogy Pty Ltd v Sino Iron Pty Ltd (No.6)* [2015] FCA 825 at [981]), this would merely reveal a difference between Australian and English law. For discussion of the Court of Appeal decision see P. Turner [2019] C.L.J. 276–279. For discussion of the Supreme Court decision and comparison with the Australian position, see N. Tiverios [2020] C.L.J. 17. For further Australian discussion of the point see, e.g. *Auburn Shopping Village Pty Ltd v Nelmeer Hoteliers Pty Ltd* [2018] NSWCA 114; 19 BPR 38569 at [25] (Bathurst CJ); *Ayers Rock SkyShip Pty Ltd v Voyages Indigenous Tourism Australia Pty Ltd* [2019] NSWSC 828 at [106]–[107] (Drake J).

(c)   Ousting of the jurisdiction by statute.

Replace n.274 with:

[274] See, e.g. LPA 1925 s.146; Commonhold and Leasehold Reform Act 2002 ss.167–170. Note too **13-030** Coronavirus Act 2020 ss.81-83.

CHAPTER 14.

INTRODUCTION

2. DISCRETION

Replace para.14-002 with:

14-002 It is sometimes said that the remedies treated in this part of the book are discretionary. The extent of the freedom the court enjoys in deciding whether to grant these remedies, as compared with the freedom it enjoys in relation to other remedies, can be overstated. It consists principally in the need to make what are sometimes fine judgments in order to apply more or less settled principles to the factual circumstances of particular cases. In some cases the description of a remedy as being discretionary only means that its principles are still being worked out.[6] To illustrate, while the decision to rescind a contract is said to be discretionary, the principles according to which that discretion must be exercised have been settled over the years through the articulation of the bars. If rescission has become barred, the court will exercise its discretion to refuse rescission. But it is well established that if restitutio in integrum is possible, and if rescission is not otherwise barred, the claimant is entitled to have the contract rescinded as of right.[7] The same is true of the jurisdiction to compel the performance of a contract, which was said over a century ago to be discretionary but "confined within well-known rules".[8] Of the discretion the court enjoys in deciding whether to grant an injunction, it has been said that "the discretion is not one to be exercised according to the fancy of whoever is to exercise the jurisdiction of equity".[9] And again in relation to the jurisdiction to order that an account of profits be taken, one finds statements that "although an account of profits, like other equitable remedies, is said to be discretionary, it is granted or withheld according to settled principles".[10] Speaking of rectification, the Court of Appeal has emphasised that albeit the origins of the remedy lie in conscience and fair dealing,its principles should be as clear and predictable in their application as possible.[10a]

[6] *Vercoe v Rutland Fund Management Limited* [2010] Bus. L.R. D141 at [340].

[47]

[7] *Lagunas Nitrate Co v Lagunas Syndicate* [1899] 2 Ch. 393 CA at 456; *Spence v Crawford* [1939] 3 All E.R. 271 HL(Sc) at 280.

[8] *Ryan v Mutual Tontine Westminster Chambers Association* [1893] 1 Ch. 116, at 126.

[9] *Doherty v Allman* (1878) 3 App.Cas. 709, at 728–29.

[10] *Warman International Ltd v Dwyer* (1995) 182 C.L.R. 544; *Goyal v Florence Care Limited* [2020] EWHC 659 (Ch) [34]-[44]. Cf. *Walsh v Shanahan* [2013] EWCA Civ 411 at [63], [66] and *Novoship (UK) Ltd v Nikitin* [2015] Q.B. 499 (CA) at [120].

[10a] *Daventry District Council v Daventry & District Housing Ltd* [2012] 1 W.L.R. 1333 CA at [194].

CHAPTER 15.

RESCISSION

3. GROUNDS

1. Misrepresentation

Replace third paragraph with:

The representee always carries the legal burden of proving inducement.[10] In the   **15-004**
case of an innocent or negligent misrepresentation, they must prove that they would
not have entered into the contract had the representation not been made.[11] In the case
of a fraudulent misrepresentation it is enough for the representee to prove that they
were materially influenced by it in the sense that it was actively present to their

mind when they decided to transact, even if there were also other reasons to have done so.[12] Inducement usually occurs where the rescinding party believes the representation to be true and acts in reliance on it, but exceptionally a fraudulent representation may induce a party to transact even though they do not believe it to be true.[13]

[10] *BV Nederlandse Industrie Van Eiprodukten v Rembrandt Enterprises Inc* [2020] Q.B. 551 CA at [15], [25].

[11] *BV Nederlandse Industrie Van Eiprodukten v Rembrandt Enterprises Inc* [2020] Q.B. 551 CA at [15]; *Assicurazioni Generali SpA v Arab insurance Group* [2003] 1 All E.R. (Comm) 140; *Pan Atlantic Insurance Co Ltd v Pine Top Insurance Co Ltd* [1995] 1 A.C. 501.

[12] *BV Nederlandse Industrie Van Eiprodukten v Rembrandt Enterprises Inc* [2020] Q.B. 551 CA at [32].

[13] *Zurich Insurance Co Plc v Hayward* [2017] A.C. 142.

Replace fourth paragraph with:

A representation is material if it would be likely to induce a person to enter a contract.[14] In cases of fraud it is not necessary that the representation was material provided inducement can be positively proved,[15] although it is open to debate whether there are circumstances in which reliance on an immaterial innocent misrepresentation will support a claim to rescind.[16] But in all cases where the representation was material, there is an evidential presumption of inducement in the sense that inducement is a natural factual inference.[17] The presumption has been said to be "very difficult to rebut" and "particularly strong where the misrepresentation was fraudulent".[18]

[14] *Smith v Chadwick* (1882) 20 Ch. D. 27 CA at 44; on appeal (1884) 9 App. Cas. 187, at 196; *BV Nederlandse Industrie Van Eiprodukten v Rembrandt Enterprises Inc* [2020] Q.B. 551 at [32].

[15] *Smith v Kay* (1859) 7 H.L.C. 750; *Pan Atlantic Insurance Co Ltd v Pine Top Insurance Co Ltd* [1995] 1 A.C. 501 at 533.

[16] See the discussion in O'Sullivan, Elliott and Zakrzewski, *The Law of Rescission*, 2nd edn (2014) [4.65]ff. It is clear that reliance on an immaterial innocent misrepresentation will not support rescission of an insurance policy: *Pan Atlantic Insurance Co Ltd v Pine Top Insurance Co Ltd* [1995] 1 A.C. 187.

[17] *Mathias v Yetts* (1882) 46 L.T. 497 CA at 502; *Smith v Land and House Property Corp* (1884) 28 Ch. D. 7 CA at 16; *Smith v Chadwick* (1884) 9 App. Cas. 187 at 196; *Barton v County NatWest Ltd* [1999] Lloyd's Rep. Bank 408 CA; *Dadourian v Simms* [2009] 1 Lloyd's Rep. 601 CA at [99]–[101]; *BV Nederlandse Industrie Van Eiprodukten v Rembrandt Enterprises Inc* [2020] Q.B. 551 CA at [32].

[18] *Zurich Insurance Co Plc v Hayward* [2017] A.C. 142 at [34], [37].

4. Fiduciary Misdealing and Bribery

After "Allied to this,", add new n.39a:

15-007 [39a] *Prince Eze v Conway* [2019] EWCA Civ 88 at [38], [43] and [63].

5. Undue Influence, Duress and Unconscionability

Replace para.15-008 with:

15-008 Rescission is available in equity in cases of undue influence and at common law in cases of duress. Undue influence may be shown to have been actually applied, or else the claimant may succeed by proving a relationship of influence, in which case a presumption of undue influence arises which it is for the defendant to rebut.[43] Duress depends on proof (a) of illegitimate pressure arising from a threat coupled with a demand; (b) that the effect of the pressure was to cause coercion in the sense of an absence of practical choice; and (c) that the pressure was a sufficient cause of the victim's entry into the transaction.[44] Pressure may be economic and may even consist in a threat to carry out a lawful act where that threat is coupled with a demand for something to which the demanding party does not in good faith consider itself entitled.[44a] Unconscionable bargains may also be rescinded,[45] as may contracts concluded by a party suffering from impaired capacity provided only that the other party knew of the impairment.[46]

[43] See Ch.8 above.

[44] *DSND Subsea Ltd v Petroleum Geoservices ASA* [2000] B.L.R. 530 at 545; *Carillion Construction Ltd v Felix (UK) Ltd* [2001] B.L.R. 1. The identification of elements in these cases has been followed in numerous subsequent cases.

[44a] *Times Travel (UK) Ltd v Pakistan International Airlines Corporation* [2020] Ch 98 CA.

[45] See Ch.8 above. Trial judges have disagreed about whether the same is true of unconscionable gifts: compare *Langton v Langton* [1995] 2 F.L.R. 890 with *Evans v Lloyd* [2013] W.T.L.R. 1137.

[46] *Hart v O'Connor* [1985] A.C. 1000 PC; *Barclays Bank Plc v Schwartz, The Times,* 2 August 1995 CA.

4. SELF-HELP RESCISSION AND JUDICIAL RESCISSION

2. Judicial Rescission

Replace n.56 with:

[56] *Erlanger v The New Sombrero Phosphate Co* (1878) 3 App. Cas. 1218 at 1278; *Spence v Crawford* **15-012** [1939] 3 All E.R. 271 HL(Sc); *O'Sullivan v Management Agency and Music Ltd* [1985] Q.B. 428 CA at [45]; cf. *Halpern v Halpern* [2008] Q.B. 195 CA.

5. EXCLUSION OF RESCISSION

2. Impossibility of Restitutio In Integrum

Replace n.77 with:

[77] *Armstrong v Jackson* [1917] 2 K.B. 822 at 829; *Salt v Stratstone Specialist Ltd (t/a Stratstone Cadil-* **15-014** *lac Newcastle)* [2016] R.L.R. 17 CA at [22].

Replace list with:

- benefits which the rescinding claimant is unable to return because of the defendant's wrongdoing[81];
- benefits the defendant was bound to confer in any event[82];
- assets that were always worthless[83]; and
- insurance premiums in certain cases[84]

[81] *Rees v De Bernardy* [1896] 2 Ch. 437, 446. Similarly, rescission will not be barred by the claimant's inability to restore the defendant to an advantageous position which they obtained through illegitimate means: *Borelli v Ting* [2010] UKPC 21 at 39.

[82] *Hulton v Hulton* [1917] 1 K.B. 813 CA.

[83] *Phosphate Sewage Co v Hartmont* (1875) 5 Ch. D. 394 CA at 454–55; *Halpern v Halpern* [2008] Q.B. 195 CA.

[84] Marine Insurance Act 1906 ss.84(1) and 84(3)(a) (marine insurance); Consumer Insurance (Disclosure and Representations) Act 2012 (consumer insurance); and Insurance Act 2015 (other non-consumer insurance).

4. Disproportionate Effect

Replace para.15-016 with:

Section 2(2) of the Misrepresentation Act 1967 confers on judges and arbitra- **15-016** tors a discretionary power, where rescission is claimed for non-fraudulent misrepresentation, to "declare the contract subsisting and award damages in lieu of rescission".[99] The power was intended to be used where the consequences for the defendant of rescission would be disproportionately hard compared with the consequences for the claimant of the contract remaining on foot, particularly where the misrepresentation relates to a fact of minor importance.[100] The power only exists where rescission would otherwise be available.[101] In effect s.2(2) creates a discretionary bar to rescission in those circumstances, coupled with a power and duty to award damages where the bar is applied. Rescission remains, however, the normal remedy and it should be awarded where possible.[102]

[99] As to the measure of damages, see para.20-060 below.

[100] Law Reform Commission, "Innocent Misrepresentation" (Cmnd. 1782, 1962) paras [11] and [12].

[101] *Salt v Stratstone Specialist Ltd (t/a Stratstone Cadillac Newcastle)* [2016] R.L.R. 17 CA at [17].

[102] *Salt v Stratstone Specialist Ltd (t/a Stratstone Cadillac Newcastle)* [2016] R.L.R. 17 CA at [24].

6. EFFECT OF RESCISSION

3. Consequential Claims and Adjustments

Replace n.120 with:

15-021 [120] *Erlanger v The New Sombrero Phosphate Co* (1878) 3 App. Cas. 1218 at 1278; the party claiming compensation or another adjustment carries the burden of proof: *Salt v Stratstone Specialist Ltd (t/a Stratstone Cadillac Newcastle)* [2016] R.L.R. 17 CA at [30].

After "is otherwise barred.", add new n.128:

[128] Affirmation may impact on causation and the measurement of loss in important ways, as to which see *Motortrak Limited v FCA Australia Pty Ltd* [2018] EWHC 1464 (Comm).

CHAPTER 16.

RECTIFICATION

1.   NATURE OF RECTIFICATION

1.   The Remedy of Rectification

(a)   The Role of Rectification.

Replace n.3 with:

[3] See *Racal Group Services v Ashmore* [1995] S.T.C. 1151 at 1154; *Allnutt v Wilding* [2007] EWCA   **16-001**
Civ 412; [2007] W.T.L.R. 941. This paragraph was cited with approval in *Univar UK Ltd v Smith* [2020]
EWHC 1596 (Ch) at [195] and *Musst Holdings Ltd v Astra Asset Management UK Ltd* [2020] EWHC
337 (Ch) at [33].

Replace n.8 with:

[8] This was approved by the Supreme Court of Canada in *Canada (Attorney General) v Fairmont Hotels
Inc* [2016] S.C.C. 56 at [13], and in *SPS Technologies Ltd v Moitt* [2020] EWHC 2421 (Ch) at [7].

(b)   Discretion.

Replace n.11 with:

[11] *Whiteside v Whiteside* [1950] Ch. 65 at 71, per Evershed MR; *Racal Group Services v Ashmore* [1995]   **16-002**
S.T.C. 1151 at 1154; *Pitt v Holt* [2013] UKSC 26; [2013] 2 A.C. 108. This was cited with approval in
SPS Technologies Ltd v Moitt [2020] EWHC 2421 (Ch) at [7].

2. Documents that will be Rectified

(b) Voluntary Instruments.

Replace n.31 with:

16-005 [31] *Day v Day* [2013] EWCA Civ 280; [2014] Ch. 114; *Merchant Navy Officers Pension Fund Trustees v Watkins* [2013] EWHC 4741 (Ch). See too *SPS Technologies Ltd v Moitt* [2020] EWHC 2421 (Ch).

(c) Wills.

Replace first para.16-006 with:

16-006 Formerly, short of fraud, there was no power to rectify a will[37]; the furthest the court could go was to omit spurious words.[38] Now, however, by statute, if a court is satisfied that a will is so expressed that it fails to carry out the intentions of the testator in consequence of a clerical error[39] or failure to understand his instructions, the court may order that the will be rectified.[40] The action for rectification cannot, without the permission of the court, be commenced later than six months after the grant of probate.[41]

[37] *Harter v Harter* (1872–75) L.R. 3 P. & D. 11; *Collins v Elstone* [1893] P. 1.

[38] *In the Goods of Schott* [1901] P. 190; *Vaughan v Clerk* (1902) 87 L.T. 144.

[39] See *Wordingham v Royal Exchange Trust Co Ltd* [1992] Ch. 412; *Re Segelman (Deceased)* [1996] Ch. 171; *Bell v Georgiou* [2002] W.T.L.R. 1105; *Brown v Bimson* [2010] All E.R. (D) 325 (Jul). Rectification was refused in *Boswell v Lawson* [2011] EWCA Civ 452, because the Court of Appeal held that the will as drafted did in fact represent the testator's intentions. See now the detailed discussion in *Marley v Rawlings* [2014] UKSC 2; [2014] 2 W.L.R. 213, which has been applied in, e.g. *Burnard v Burnard* [2014] EWHC 340 (Ch); *Brooke v Purton* [2014] EWHC 547 (Ch); *Reading v Reading* [2015] EWHC 946 (Ch); The action for rectification cannot, without the permission of the court, be commenced later than six months after the grant of probate*Kelly v Brennan* [2020] EWHC 245 (Ch).

[40] Administration of Justice Act 1982 s.20(1), applying where the testator has died after 1982 (see ss.73(1), 76(11)).

[41] Administration of Justice Act 1982 s.20(2). For the principles to be applied by the court in extending time, see *Re Chittock (Deceased)* [2000] W.T.L.R. 643; *Kelly v Brennan* [2020] EWHC 245 (Ch).

2. SCOPE OF RECTIFICATION

(a) Interpretation.

Replace n.54 with:

16-008 [54] See *Investors Compensation Scheme Ltd v West Bromwich Building Society* [1998] 1 W.L.R. 896 HL at 912 (Lord Hoffmann's third principle). See too *MV Promotions Limited and Micheal Vaughan v Telegraph Media Group Limited and HMRC* [2020] EWHC 1537 (Ch) at [66].

3. MISTAKE

1. Common Mistake

(a) Prior Agreement.

Replace first paragraph with:

16-014 The prior agreement between the parties on which a claim for rectification is based need not amount to an enforceable contract; it suffices if there is a common intention in regard to the particular provisions of the agreement in question[90] continuing up to the date of the written instrument,[91] together with some outward expression of accord.[92] This requirement of an "outward expression of accord" was once thought to serve only an evidentiary function[93] but is now treated as a legal requirement.[94] However, no outward expression of accord is required proceedings for the rectification of a pension scheme,[94a] in cases where the instrument is not intended to set out an accord between two or more parties (i.e. if the underlying transaction is unilateral); nor where a unilateral transaction requires the consent of another.

[90] *Joscelyne v Nissen* [1970] 2 Q.B. 86; applying *Crane v Hegeman-Harris Co Inc* [1939] 1 All E.R. 662; [1971] 3 All E.R. 245n.; [1971] 1 W.L.R. 1390n. (affirmed [1939] 4 All E.R. 68); and not following dicta in *Lovell and Christmas Ltd v Wall* (1911) 104 L.T. 85; and *Frederick E Rose (London) Ltd v William H. Pim Jnr & Co Ltd* [1953] 2 Q.B. 450. See also *Monaghan CC v Vaughan* [1948] I.R. 306; *Slee v Warke* (1952) 86 C.L.R. 271 at 280, 281.

[91] *Crane v Hegeman Harris Co Inc* [1939] 1 All E.R. 662.

[92] *Joscelyne v Nissen* [1970] Q.B. 86 at 98, criticised by L. Bromley, "Rectification in Equity" (1971) 87 L.Q.R. 532.

[93] *Munt v Beasley* [2006] EWCA Civ 370 at [36], per Mummery LJ.

[94] *FSHC Group Holdings Ltd v Glas Trust Corp Ltd* [2019] EWCA Civ 1361 at [75]–[77].

[94a] *Univar UK Ltd v Smith* [2020] EWHC 1596 (Ch) at [205]-[207]; *Re Colart Pension Scheme* [2020] Pens. L.R. 3 at [7]; *Re Chas A Blatchford & Sons Ltd Group Pension Scheme* [2019] EWHC 2743 (Ch); *Lloyds Bank Plc v Lloyds Banking Group Pensions Trustees Ltd* [2019] EWHC 3775 (Ch); *SPS Technologies Ltd v Moitt* [2020] EWHC 2421 (Ch). See too *FSHC Group Holdings Ltd v Glas Trust Corp Ltd* [2019] EWCA Civ 1361 [78]–[79]. No outward manifestation of an accord is required in cases where the instrument is not intended to set out an accord between two or more parties (i.e. if the underlying transaction is unilateral); nor where a unilateral transaction requires the consent of another: *AMP (UK) Plc v Barker* [2001] Pens. L.R. 77; followed in *Gallaher Ltd v Gallaher Pensions Ltd* [2005] EWHC 42 (Ch); [2005] Pens. L.R. 103.

(b) Continuing Intention.

Replace n.118 with:

[118] *FSHC Group Holdings Ltd v Glas Trust Corp Ltd* [2019] EWCA Civ 136 at [176]; noted Davies [2020] C.L.J. 8; Peel (2020) 136 L.Q.R. 205.. The outward expression of accord must exist at the time of the contract: *Musst Holdings Ltd v Astra Asset Management UK Ltd* [2020] EWHC 337 (Ch).   **16-015**

(c) Failure to Represent Agreement.

Replace n.123 with:

[123] *Giles v Royal National Institute for the Blind* [2014] EWHC 1373; *Lee v Lee* [2018] EWHC 149 (Ch). This paragraph was cited with approval in *Musst Holdings Ltd v Astra Asset Management UK Ltd* [2020] EWHC 337 (Ch) at [33].   **16-016**

2. Unilateral Mistake

(d) Unilateral transactions.

Replace n.165 with:

[165] See *Wright v Goff* (1856) 22 Beav. 207 at 214. This paragraph was cited with approval in *Re Webster* [2020] EWHC 2275 (Ch) at [37], [46]-[48], where the judge thought a unilateral tax return submitted by a taxpayer as a consequence of a statutory requirement was not capable of rectification (and would not have granted rectification anyway).   **16-021**

4. DEFENCES

1. Valid Defences

After "equitable and discretionary.", add new n.192a:

16-025   [192a] *MV Promotions Limited and Micheal Vaughan v Telegraph Media Group Limited and HMRC* [2020] EWHC 1537 (Ch).

Replace n.201 with:

[201] See *Whiteside v Whiteside* [1950] Ch. 65 CA, where the parties had already entered into a supplementary deed rectifying the error before the matter came to court. See also *Racal Group Services Ltd v Ashmore* [1995] S.T.C. 1151 at 1158, per Peter Gibson LJ; *MV Promotions Limited and Micheal Vaughan v Telegraph Media Group Limited and HMRC* [2020] EWHC 1537 (Ch). However in *Giles v Royal National Institute for the Blind* [2014] EWHC 1373 (Ch) it was no bar to rectification (of a deed of variation of a will) that in executing the deed it was the claimant's objective to relieve the beneficiaries of the indirect burden of inheritance tax.

CHAPTER 17.

SPECIFIC PERFORMANCE

2. INADEQUACY OF DAMAGES—THRESHOLD REQUIREMENT FOR AVAILABILITY OF
SPECIFIC PERFORMANCE

1. General Principles and Trends

Replace n.37 with:

[37] In *Anders Utkilens Rederi A/S v O/Y Lovisa Stevedoring Co A/B and Keller Bryant Transport Co* **17-007**
[1985] 2 All E.R. 669 at 674 Goulding J said: "Commercial life would be subjected to new and unjust
hazards if the court were to decree specific performance of contracts normally sounding only in damages simply because of a party's threatened insolvency. Thus I cannot accept the argument based simply
on financial instability". The Court of Appeal has declined to order specific performance by analogy with
the principle that a claimant will be denied cost of cure damages but will be confined to damages for
loss of amenity if it would be "disproportionate" to cure the breach (*Ruxley Electronics and Construction Ltd v Forsyth* [1996] A.C. 344; [1995] 2 All E.R. 268; [1995] 3 W.L.R. 118). In *Newman v
Framewood Manor Management Co Ltd* [2012] EWCA Civ 159, the court denied specific performance
of a landlord's covenant to provide a jacuzzi, where a sauna had been provided instead. As Arden LJ
said, "In my judgment, the judge was correct not to award a specific performance. To incur this cost
would be excessive and disproportionate when compared with the loss of amenity".

2. Specific Examples

(a) Land.

After "potential with no intention", insert:

17-008   of residing there,

(b) Chattels.

Replace second paragraph with:

17-009   The Sale of Goods Act[50] has widened this remedy slightly by giving the court, in the case of non-consumer sale of goods contracts, a discretion to order specific performance of a contract to deliver "specific or ascertained goods" without giving the seller the option of retaining the goods and paying damages.[51] In practice, the courts are reluctant to exercise this discretion unless the goods are effectively unique.[52] However, in very exceptional circumstances in which the normal market is not functioning, the courts may be more flexible about specific remedies, even for goods that are not specific or ascertained. In *Sky Petroleum Ltd v VIP Petroleum Ltd*,[53] the plaintiff had a 10-year contract with the defendant under which the plaintiff undertook to obtain all the petrol and diesel required for its filling stations from the defendant. During the oil crisis, the defendant purported to terminate the agreement in breach of contract and, exceptionally, Goulding J was prepared to grant an interlocutory injunction restraining this breach, even though this had the indirect effect of compelling the defendant to supply the petrol and diesel, because the unusual state of the market meant that the plaintiff had little prospect of finding an alternative supply and would otherwise be forced out of business.

[50]   As amended by the Consumer Rights Act 2015.

[51]   See Sale of Goods Act 1979 s.52(1) (jurisdiction), s.61(1) (meaning of "specific"); and see *Re Wait* [1927] 1 Ch. 606 (on "ascertained"); and *Cohen v Roche* [1927] 1 K.B. 169 (power to order specific performance is discretionary). For the regime for consumer contracts, see now Pt I of the Consumer Rights Act 2015.

[52]   *Cohen v Roche* [1927] 1 K.B. 169; *Gregor Fisken Ltd v Carl* [2020] EWHC 1385 (Comm).

[53]   *Sky Petroleum Ltd v VIP Petroleum Ltd* [1974] 1 W.L.R. 576; considered in *Land Rover Group Ltd v UPF (UK) Ltd (in Administrative Receivership)* [2002] EWHC 3183 (QB); and *VTB Commodities Trading DAC v JSC Antipinsky Refinery* [2020] EWHC 72 (Comm).

(d) Money.

After "be specifically enforced.", add new n.62a:

17-011   [62a]   Paragraph 17-011 was cited with approval by Picken J in *Avonwick Holdings Ltd v Azitio Holdings Ltd* [2020] EWHC 1844 (Comm).

3. Bars to Specific Performance

1. The Nature of the Contractual Obligation

(a) Contracts involving personal service.

(1) Employment contracts.

Replace n.80 with:

17-013   [80]   *Johnson v Shrewsbury and Birmingham Rly Co* (1853) 3 De. G.M. & G. 914, where Knight Bruce LJ said, "We are asked to compel one person to employ against his will another as his confidential servant, for duties with respect to the due performance of which the utmost confidence is required. Let him be one of the best and most competent persons that ever lived, still if the two do not agree, and good people do not always agree, enormous mischief may be done". Lord Wilson in *Geys v Societe Generale* [2012] UKSC 63, [2013] 1 A.C. 523, noted that, "The big question whether nowadays the more impersonal, less hierarchical, relationship of many employers with their employees requires review of the usual unavailability of specific performance has been raised ... but is beyond the scope of this appeal."

2. The Relevance of Other Contractual Obligations

(a) Mutuality.

Replace n.174 with:

[174] Buckley LJ in *Price v Strange* [1978] Ch. 337 at 367–368. For an argument that even this formula-tion affords undue protection to defendants, see A. Burrows, *Remedies for Torts and Breach of Contract*, 4th edn (Oxford: Oxford University Press, 2019), p.427.   **17-024**

3. Other Reasons for Refusing Specific Performance

(d) Misdescription.

(1) Substantial misdescription.

After "the misdescription is", replace "to prevent the purchaser from really getting the property which he bought," with:

that the purchaser will not in reality be acquiring the property which he intended to purchase,   **17-035**

(2) Slight misdescription.

Replace second paragraph with:

The principle of granting specific performance with compensation is not one to be extended, and will never be applied in an action by the vendor to enforce the contract where he has been guilty of fraud or wilful[234] misrepresentation.[235] Nor will the court apply this principle at the suit of either party if the proper amount of compensation cannot be ascertained.[236] Further, a standard condition is commonly inserted in contracts for the sale of land to the effect that the lots are believed to be correctly described, but that errors shall not annul the sale and that no compensa-tion shall be paid for or in respect of any misdescription.[237] Notwithstanding such a condition, however, the purchaser may treat the contract as repudiated and terminate it if the misdescription is fraudulent or, though not fraudulent, is on a material and substantial point so that, but for the misdescription, the purchaser would not have entered into the contract.[238] Any clause purporting to exclude li-ability for misrepresentation in a non-consumer contract is subject to a test of reasonableness pursuant to s.3 of the Misrepresentation Act 1967. In *Schyde Invest-ments Ltd v Cleaver*,[239] the Court of Appeal applied this test to cl.7.1.3 of the Standard Conditions of Sale, holding that the vendor had not established that the clause was a reasonable one to have included in the contract at the time when it had been made, and it was thus unenforceable.[240] Likewise, this sort of condition will fall within the Consumer Rights Act 2015 if the contract is a consumer contract (between a commercial seller and a consumer purchaser), and thus be subject to a test of fairness.   **17-036**

[234] Quaere whether wilful misrepresentation here differs from fraud.

235 See *Price v Macaulay* (1852) 2 De G.M. & G. 339 at 344.

236 *Lord Brooke v Rounthwaite* (1846) 5 Hare 298 (vendor's action); *Rudd v Lascelles* [1900] 1 Ch. 815 (purchaser's action).

237 See in particular clause 7.1.3 of the Standard Conditions of Sale.

238 *Flight v Booth* (1834) 1 Bing. N.C. 370; *Jacobs v Revell* [1900] 2 Ch. 858; *Lee v Rayson* [1917] 1 Ch. 613; *Walker v Boyle* [1982] 1 W.L.R. 495.

239 *Schyde Investments Ltd v Cleaver* [2011] EWCA Civ 929. The purchaser was seeking rescission of the contract for misrepresentation, the vendor resisted on the basis of cl.7.1.3 and counterclaimed for specific performance which was denied. See also *Cremdean Properties Ltd v Nash* (1977) 241 E.G. 837.

240 Longmore LJ emphasised that: "the question is not whether the clause is, in general, a reasonable clause. The question is whether it was a reasonable clause in the contract made between *this* vendor and *this* purchaser at the time when the contract was made".

(e)   Default by the claimant.

Replace n.252 with:

17-038   252 *Bellamy v Debenham* [1891] 1 Ch. 412; *Pips (Leisure Productions) Ltd v Walton* (1982) 43 P. & C.R. 415; *Pinekerry Ltd v Needs Ltd* (1992) 64 P. & C.R. 245. In *Dreams Ltd v Pavilion Property Trustees Ltd* [2020] EWHC 1169 (Ch), the tenant was in breach of a condition in a surrender agreement to give vacant possession, so the landlord was not required to accept the surrender without vacant possession and the tenant was denied specific performance.

(h)   Delay.

Replace para.17-044 with:

17-044   Even where time is not of the essence of the contract, specific performance may be barred by the claimant's unreasonable delay in seeking the remedy, under the equitable doctrine of laches.302 The period of delay which will bar a claim to specific performance is to be judged by equitable principles, since an action for specific performance is not sufficiently like an action for damages for breach of contract for the six year limitation period in the Limitation Act to be applicable by analogy.303 The traditional test for laches was relatively strict: for a claimant to obtain specific performance, he must have shown himself "ready, desirous, prompt, and eager".304 In practice, however, the courts show some flexibility in assessing the extent, impact of and reasons for the delay, when whether to permit specific performance. So where the claimant has been let into possession under the contract and has obtained the equitable interest, so that all he requires is a mere conveyance of the legal estate, even many years' delay in enforcing his claim will not prejudice him.305 Moreover, delay in proceeding to trial after the commencement of proceedings will not be fatal unless the defendant is led to believe that only damages are being sought.306 But even a short delay might preclude specific performance if the subject-matter of the contract is of fluctuating value. Overall, it has been suggested that delay alone is not sufficient to bar specific performance, unless the defendant has been prejudiced by the delay.307

302 *Mills v Haywood* (1877) 6 Ch. D. 196; and see *Walker v Jeffreys* (1842) 1 Hare 341; *Cornwell v Henson* [1900] 2 Ch. 298; *Behzadi v Shaftesbrury Hotels* [1992] Ch. 1 at 12.

303 If a statutory limitation provision (properly interpreted) applies to a claim, then equity will apply it in obedience to the statute; and even where the limitation period does not apply to the claim (because the claim is for an exclusively equitable remedy) the limitation will be applied by analogy if the equitable remedy is "correspondent to the remedy at law": see *P & O Nedlloyd BV v Arab Metals Co* [2006] EWCA Civ 1717 at [34]–[38], per Moore-Bick LJ. However, the remedy of specific performance is not correspondent to any common law remedy; so that no period of limitation applies by analogy at [44]– [52], per Moore-Bick LJ. *P & O Nedlloyd* was applied by Picken J in *Avonwick Holdings Ltd v Azitio Holdings Ltd* [2020] EWHC 72 (Comm) at [1091] – [1096]. Whether a statutory period of limitation

should be applied by analogy to claims for monetary relief in lieu of specific performance remains uncertain.

[304] *Milward v Earl Thanet* (1801) 5 Ves. 720n., per Arden MR; repeated by Cotton LJ in *Mills v Haywood* (1877) 6 Ch. D. 196 at 202.

[305] *Crofton v Ormsby* (1806) 2 Sch. & Lef. 583, at 603; *Shepheard v Walker* (1875) L.R. 20 Eq. 659; *Williams v Greatrex* [1957] 1 W.L.R. 31; *Frawley v Neill, The Times,* 5 April 1999; cf. *Mills v Haywood* (1877) 6 Ch. D. 196. The sentence in the text was cited in *Voyce v Voyce* (1991) 62 P. & C.R. 290 at 293 per Dillon LJ.

[306] *Du Sautoy v Symes* [1967] Ch. 1146. See also *Easton v Brown* [1981] 3 All E.R. 278 (eight years' delay after decree).

[307] Megarry VC in *Lazard Brothers & Co v Fairfield Properties Co (Mayfair) Ltd* (1977) 121 S.J. 793. See also *Taylor v Crotty* [2006] EWCA Civ 1364, where specific performance was ordered despite a delay: the delay was in part caused by the defendant denying the validity of the exercise of the option and where the defendant was "unable to point to any prejudice or equity that has arisen, which would be a ground for denying to the tenant the right to performance of the contract". See further *Avonwick Holdings Ltd v Azitio Holdings Ltd* [2020] EWHC 72 (Comm).

(i) Great hardship.

Replace fourth paragraph with:

In contrast, the fact that one party has made a poor bargain,[318] or that he is impecunious[319] or financially unable to complete, is not hardship,[320] nor is inadequacy of price a ground for refusing specific performance,[321] unless the purchaser stands in a fiduciary position to the vendor, or enters into the contract as a result of fraud.[322] Nevertheless, occasionally the court may deny specific performance because of commercial hardship. In one case specific performance of an agreement to sell land to a railway company for the purposes of its undertaking was refused after the company had abandoned the project, for the decree would have worked more injustice than justice.[323] More recently, where a flat had purportedly been sold by an agent for the vendor to one party and by the vendor personally to the claimants, thereby generating years of litigation, the Privy Council decided that specific performance of the contract with the claimants would be "wholly unworkable in practice and a recipe for yet further litigation" as well as conflicting with the overriding objective in civil proceedings of dealing with cases justly.[324] Finally, the defendant's financial difficulties might be taken into account when denying specific performance, when coupled with other factors. In one case, the defendant's financial circumstances made compliance with an obligation to build a roundabout pursuant to a development agreement nigh on impossible, whilst difficulties in obtaining planning permission for the development meant that the need for a roundabout was uncertain: in the circumstances the court thought it arguable that the defendant could defend an action for specific performance and declined summary judgment to the claimant.[325]

17-045

[318] *Adams v Weare* (1784) 1 Bro.C.C. 567; *Roberts v O'Neill* [1983] I.R. 47 (great increase in value of land after contract).

[319] *RVB Investments Ltd v Bibby* [2013] EWHC 65 (Ch).

[320] *Nicholas v Ingram* [1958] N.Z.L.R. 972. And see *Francis v Cowcliff, The Times,* 30 March 1976 (landlord's financial inability to provide and maintain a lift). See also *Francis v Vista Del Mar Development Ltd (Cayman Islands)* [2019] UKPC 14.

[321] In *Mountford v Scott* [1975] Ch. 258, where an option was granted to the purchaser to purchase the vendor's house for less than its value, the Court of Appeal rejected the vendor's argument that specific performance should not be ordered: "If the owner of a house contracts with his eyes open ... it cannot in my view be right to deny specific performance to the purchaser because the vendor then finds it difficult to find a house to buy that suits him and his family on the basis of the amount of money in the proceeds of sale".

[322] *Coles v Trecothick* (1804) 9 Ves. 234 at 246: *Sullivan v Jacob* (1828) 1 Moll. 472 at 477.

[323] *Webb v Direct London & Portsmouth Ry Co* (1852) I De G.M. & G. 521 at 529, 530.

[324] *O'Connor v Piccott* [2010] UKPC 4.

[325] *North East Lincolnshire BC v Millennium Park (Grimsby) Ltd* [2002] EWCA Civ 1719.

INJUNCTION

1.   INTRODUCTION

3.   Jurisdiction

(a)   Courts.

Replace n.25 with:

[25] See para.1-038. Moreover, all courts may grant injunctions under the Human Rights Act: *Re G* **18-005** *(Children)* [2019] EWCA Civ 1779; [2020] 1 F.L.R. 391.

(c) Parties.

Replace n.35 with:

18-007 [35] *Secretary of State for the Environment, Food and Rural Affairs v Meier* [2009] UKSC 11; [2009] 1 W.L.R. 2780. See also *South Cambridgeshire DC v Persons Unknown* [2004] EWCA Civ 1280; [2004] 4 P.L.R. 88; *Bloomsbury Publishing Plc v Newsgroup Newspapers Ltd* [2003] EWHC 1087 (Ch); [2003] 1 W.L.R. 1633; *Vastint Leeds B.V. v Persons Unknown* [2018] EWHC 2456 (Ch) at [19]–[25] (Marcus Smith J); *Boyd v Ineos Upstream Ltd* [2019] EWCA Civ 515; J. Seymour, "Injunctions enjoining non-parties: distinction without difference?" (2007) 66 C.L.J. 605. See too *Olympic Delivery Authority v Persons Unknown* [2012] EWHC 1012 (Ch); *Cameron v Liverpool Victoria Insurance Co Ltd* [2019] UKSC 6; [2019] 1 W.L.R. 1471; *Cuadrilla Bowland Ltd v Persons Unknown* [2020] EWCA Civ 9; [2020] 4 W.L.R. 29; *Canada Goose UK Retail Ltd v Persons Unknown* [2020] EWCA Civ 303; [2020] 1 W.L.R. 2802; *Bromley LBC v Persons Unknown* [2020] EWCA Civ 12; *Birmingham City Council v Afsar* [2020] EWHC 864 (QB); [2020] E.L.R. 341.

2. PERPETUAL (OR FINAL) INJUNCTIONS

2. Rights which, if Infringed, may Justify the Grant of a Final Injunction

Replace n.64 with:

18-011 [64] See Ch.30. In *AA v Persons Unknown* [2019] EWHC 3556 (Comm); [2020] 4 W.L.R. 35 Bryan J. held that cryptocurrencies were a form of property and could be subject to proprietary injunctions.

(a) Real property rights.

(1) Trespass.

Replace n.67 with:

18-012 [67] *Patel v WH Smith (Eziot) Ltd* [1987] 1 W.L.R. 853. A hospital is no different from any other landowner when seeking injunctive relief against patients: *University College London Hospitals Foundation Trust v MB* [2020] EWHC 882 (QB).

(b) Intellectual property rights.

Replace n.105 with:

18-016 [105] *L'Oréal SA v eBay International AG Case C-324/09* [2012] All E.R. (EC) 501; *UPC Telekabel Wien GmbH v Constantin Film Verleih GmbH Case C-314/12* [2014] E.C.D.R. 12. See too, e.g. *Dramatico Entertainment Ltd v British Sky Broadcasting Ltd* [2012] EWHC 268 (Ch); [2012] 3 C.M.L.R. 14; *Twentieth Century Fox Film Corp v Newzbin Ltd* [2010] EWHC 608 (Ch); [2010] E.C.C. 13. For further discussion in the context of "blocking injunctions" see *Cartier International AG v British Telecommunications Plc* [2018] UKSC 28; [2018] 1 W.L.R. 3259; *Nintendo Co Ltd v Sky UK Ltd* [2019] EWHC 2376 (Ch); [2020] 3 All E.R. 83.

3. The Equity to Grant Injunctive Relief

(d) The discretion to refuse relief.

(4) Hardship.

Replace n.284 with:

18-040 [284] *Pride of Derby and Derbyshire Angling Assoc Ltd v British Celanese Ltd* [1953] Ch. 149. *In Priyanka Shipping Ltd v Glory Bulk Carriers Pte Ltd* [2019] EWHC 2804 (Comm); [2019] 1 W.L.R. 6677 at [91] "inconvenience or hardship" was held to be an insufficient reason to refuse injunctive relief; although an injunction may be refused if it would be "unconscionable" or "oppressive", and the may take into account the adequacy of damages: [97].

4. Damages in Substitution for (or Addition to) Injunction

Replace fourth paragraph with:

However, this traditional understanding of the law[322] may no longer be **18-044** appropriate. In *Coventry v Lawrence*,[323] the Supreme Court signalled a move away from the *Shelfer* guidelines on the basis that they were "out-dated"[324] and that the broad discretion of the court in this area should not be restricted by a mechanical test.[324a] It may therefore be expected that courts will show a greater willingness to take into account the public interest, and that a broader approach will generally be taken by the courts when deciding whether or not to award damages in lieu of an injunction, even if the defendant still bears a "legal burden" to show why an injunction should not be granted.[325] But even within a wider approach, the factors raised in *Shelfer* are likely to remain relevant as the courts attempt to determine the correct test to apply when considering whether there should be an injunction or damages in lieu.[326]

[322] The preceding paragraph was cited with approval by Morgan J in *Loveluck-Edwards v Ideal Developments Ltd* [2012] EWHC 716 (Ch); [2012] 2 P. & C.R. DG2 at [114].

[323] *Coventry v Lawrence* [2014] UKSC 13; [2014] A.C. 822.

[324] It should be noted that the "working rule" of *Shelfer* [1895] 1 Ch. 287 CA is not necessarily exhaustive, and there may be other situations in which damages may be awarded in lieu of an injunction, e.g. *Jaggard v Sawyer* [1995] 1 W.L.R. 269, 287, per Millett LJ.

[324a] In *Unwired Planet International Ltd v Huawei Technologies (UK) Co Ltd* [2020] UKSC 37 at [162] the Supreme Court approved of Lord Neuberger's approach in Coventry v Lawrence and held that "the court's power to award damages in lieu of an injunction involves a classic exercise of discretion".

[325] *Coventry v Lawrence* [2014] UKSC 13; [2014] A.C. 822 at [121] (Lord Neuberger).

[326] See, e.g. *Higson v Guenault* [2014] EWCA Civ 703 [51] (Aikens LJ).); *Priyanka Shipping Ltd v Glory Bulk Carriers Pte Ltd* [2019] EWHC 2804 (Comm); [2019] 1 W.L.R. 6677. For further discussion see, e.g. *Prophet Plc v Huggett* [2014] EWHC 615 (Ch); [2014] I.R.L.R. 618 at [26]–[28] (not considered on appeal: [2014] EWCA Civ 1013; [2014] I.R.L.R. 797); *Comic Enterprise Ltd v Twentieth Century Fox Film Corp* [2014] EWHC 2286 (Ch); [2014] E.T.M.R. 51; *Kerry Ingredients (UK) Ltd v Bakkavor Group Ltd* [2016] EWHC 2448 (Ch) at [74]ff; *Ottercroft Ltd v Scandia Care Ltd* [2016] EWCA Civ 867; *Apexmaster Ltd v URC Thames North Trust* [2018] 2 WLUK 584 [71]–[83]; *Business Mortgage Finance 6 Plc v Greencoat Investments Ltd* [2019] EWHC 2128 (Ch) [96]–[102]; *Beaumont Business Centres Ltd v Florala Properties Ltd* [2020] EWHC 550 (Ch).

3. INTERIM INJUNCTIONS

2. The Jurisdiction to Grant Interim Injunctions

(b) Arbitrations.

Replace n.344 with:

[344] Arbitration Act 1996 s.44(4). For discussion of this provision and s.43(3) when the matter has ceased **18-048** to be urgent see *VTB Commodities Trading DAC v JSC Antipinsky Refinery v Petraco Oil Co SA* [2020] EWHC 72 (Comm); [2020] 1 W.L.R. 1227.

3. Enforcement of Substantive Rights Pending Trial—Prohibitory Injunctions

(b) The principles to be applied.

(1) Serious question.

Replace n.358 with:

18-052   [358] *Cayne v Global Natural Resources Plc* [1984] 1 All E.R. 225. A majority of the Court of Appeal recently held that an injunction could be granted to enforce an injunction or undertaking: *Koza Ltd. & Hamdi Akin Ipek v Koza Altin Isletmeleri AS* [2020] EWCA Civ 1018.

(5) Special factors.

Replace n.374 with:

18-056   [374] *Smith v Inner London Education Authority* [1978] 1 All E.R. 411. See too *R. (on the application of the Press Standards Board of Finance Ltd) v Secretary of State for Culture, Media and Sport* [2013] EWHC 3824 (Admin) (no interim injunction to restrain the Secretary of State from placing any charter regarding press regulation before the Privy Council). Indeed, the public interest is important whenever a public authority is involved: *R. (The Governing Body of X) v Office for Standards in Education, Children's Services and Skills* [2020] EWCA Civ 594; [2020] E.M.L.R. 22.

5. Preventing the Dissipation of Assets—Freezing Orders

(a) Origins.

Replace n.493 with:

18-070   [493] See SCA 1981 s.37(3) which recognises the court's power to make such orders. In *UL v BK* [2013] EWHC 1735 (Fam); [2014] Fam. 35 at [9]–[14], Mostyn J expressed the view that power to grant a freezing injunction arises from the inherent equitable jurisdiction of the court. For the County Court's jurisdiction, see para.18-015. CPR PD 25 para.1 enables Masters or District Judges to make freezing orders in certain circumstances. Freezing orders can also be granted by the Patents County Court: *Suh v Ryu* [2012] EWPCC 20; [2012] F.S.R 31. The breadth of s.37 was recognized in *Koza Ltd. & Hamdi Akin Ipek v Koza Altin Isletmeleri AS* [2020] EWCA Civ 1018.

(d) Guidelines.

(1) Disclosure.

Replace n.513 with:

18-074   [513] *Memory Corp Plc v Sidhu (No.2)* [2000] 1 W.L.R. 1443 at 1455. See also *Brink's Mat Ltd v Elcombe* [1988] 1 W.L.R. 1350; *Behbehani v Salem (Note)* [1989] 1 W.L.R. 723; *Dadourian Group International Inc v Sims* [2007] EWHC 1673 (Ch); *JSC Commercial Bank Privatbank v Kolomoisky* [2019] EWCA Civ 1708; [2020] 2 W.L.R. 993.

(4) Risk of removal or dissipation.

Replace para.18-077 with:

18-077   "Dissipation" includes disposition, pledges and charges.[532] However, it does not include handing an asset over to the owner of that asset[533]; nor does it include the right to borrow, the exercise of which is not equivalent to the disposal of an asset.[534] The court will consider whether the dissipation was unjustifiable.[535] It is essential that there be a real risk of the assets being removed or dissipated before the judgment is satisfied[536] : a freezing order will not be granted merely to provide claimants with security, even where this could be done without causing hardship to the defendant.[537]

[532] *CBS UK v Lambert* [1983] Ch. 37; *Z Ltd v A-Z* [1982] 1 Q.B. 558. Both these cases drew upon the language of "otherwise dealing with" in Senior Courts Act 1981 s.37(3). In *Taylor v Van Dutch Marine Holding Ltd* [2017] EWHC 636 (Ch) Mann J held (disapproving *Gangway Ltd v Caledonian Park Investments (Jersey) Ltd* [2001] 2 Lloyd's Rep. 715) that a third-party's enforcing a charge over property which is frozen by the freezing order would not be an act prohibited by the order.

[533] *The Law Society v Shanks* [1988] 1 F.L.R. 504; departing from the speech of Lord Denning in *Z Ltd v A-Z* [1982] 1 Q.B. 558. *Mobil Cerro Negro Ltd v Petroleos de Venezuela SA* [2008] EWHC 532 (Comm); [2008] 2 All E.R. (Comm) 1034 held that the dissipation must be by conduct that is unjustifiable. See too *Fundo Soberano de Angola v dos Santos* [2018] EWHC 2199 (Comm); *Lakatamia Shipping Company Limited v Morimoto* [2019] EWCA Civ 2203; *Organic Grape Spirit Limited v Nueva IQT, S.L.* [2020] EWCA Civ 999.

[534] *JSC BTA Bank v Ablyazov* [2015] UKSC 64; [2015] 1 W.L.R. 4754.

[535] *Candy v Holyoake* [2017] EWCA Civ 92; [2017] 2 All E.R. (Comm) 513; see too *Claremont Group Interiors v Boultbee (Marlybone) Ltd* [2018] EWHC 3886 (TCC).

[536] *Z Ltd v A-Z* [1982] 1 Q.B. 558; *Thane Investments Ltd v Tomlinson* [2003] EWCA Civ 1272; *JSC BTA Bank v Ablyazov* [2015] UKSC 64; [2015] 1 W.L.R. 4754; *Congentra AG v Sixteen Thirteen Marine SA (The Nicholas M)* [2008] EWHC 1615 (Comm); [2009] 1 All E.R. (Comm) 479; *IOT Engineering Projects Ltd v Dangote Fertilizer Ltd* [2014] EWCA Civ 1348; *Lakatamia Shipping Company Limited v Morimoto* [2019] EWCA Civ 2203; *Crowther v Crowther* [2020] EWCA Civ 762.

[537] *Ninemia Maritime Corp v Trave Schiffahrtsgesellschaft mbH und Co KG* [1983] 1 W.L.R. 1412; *Refco v Eastern Trading Co* [1999] 1 Lloyd's Rep. 159. In *Candy v Holyoake* [2017] EWCA Civ 92; [2017] 2 All E.R. (Comm) 513 the Court of Appeal considered that the same considerations apply to notification injunctions as to freezing injunctions, and considered the correct test in relation to risk of dissipation (at [34]–[48]).

(e) Form of order.

(5) *Permissible expenses.*

Replace n.548 with:

[548] *AJ Bekhor & Co v Bilton* [1981] Q.B. 923; *PCW (Underwriting Agencies) Ltd v Dixon* [1983] 2 All **18-085** E.R. 158, 697n; *Avant Petroleum Inc v Gatoil Overseas Inc* [1986] 2 Lloyd's Rep. 236. Pre-existing standard of living expenses are permissible, but the court should not speculate about future expenses: *Vneshprombank LLC v Bedzhamov* [2019] EWCA Civ 1992.

(g) Worldwide freezing orders.

Replace n.572 with:

[572] Brussels I Regulation (recast) (1215/2012) art.10. For discussion of the scope of this provision (which **18-088** mirrors art.31 of the old Brussels I Regulation (44/2001)), see *Masri v Consolidated Contractors International (UK) Ltd* [2008] EWCA Civ 876; [2009] 2 W.L.R. 699, although the European aspects of the case did not need to be considered by the House of Lords: [2009] UKHL 43; [2010] 1 A.C. 90. For an interesting discussion of whether a worldwide freezing order granted in another member state and recognised in England under art.38 of the old Brussels I Regulation is effective immediately or only after a period of time, and whether "measures of enforcement" under art.47(3) includes service of the worldwide freezing order, see *Cyprus Popular Bank Public Co Ltd v Vgenopoulos* [2018] EWCA Civ 1; [2018] Q.B. 886. For the future of this Regulation, see fn. 626.

Replace n.577 with:

[577] *Dadourian Group International Inc v Simms* [2006] EWCA Civ 399; [2006] 1 W.L.R. 2499 identified eight "guidelines": (1) The principle applying to the grant of permission to enforce a WFO abroad is that the grant of that permission should be just and convenient for the purpose of ensuring the effectiveness of the WFO, and that it is not oppressive to the parties to the English proceedings or to third parties who may be joined in the foreign proceedings. (2) All the relevant circumstances and options need to be considered. In particular consideration should be given to granting relief on terms, e.g. terms as to the extension to third parties of the undertaking to compensate for costs incurred as a result of the WFO and as to the type of proceedings that may be commenced abroad. Consideration should also be given to the proportionality of the steps proposed to be taken abroad, as well as the form of any order. (3) The interests of the applicant should be balanced against the interests of the other parties to the proceedings and any new party likely to be joined to the foreign proceedings. (4) Permission should not normally be given in terms that would enable the applicant to obtain relief in the foreign proceedings which is superior to the relief given by the WFO. (5) The evidence in support of the application for

permission should contain all the information (so far as it can reasonably be obtained in the time available) necessary to enable the judge to reach an informed decision, including evidence as to the applicable law and practice in the foreign court, evidence as to the nature of the proposed proceedings to be commenced and evidence as to the assets believed to be located in the jurisdiction of the foreign court and the names of the parties by whom such assets are held. (6) The standard of proof as to the existence of assets that are both within the WFO and within the jurisdiction of the foreign court is a real prospect, i.e. the applicant must show that there is a real prospect that such assets are located within the jurisdiction of the foreign court in question. (7) There must be evidence of a risk of dissipation of the assets in question. (8) Normally the application should be made on notice to the respondent; but in cases of urgency, where it is just to do so, permission may be given without notice to the party against whom relief will be sought in the foreign proceedings—but in such cases the party should have the earliest practicable opportunity of having the matter reconsidered by the court at a hearing of which he is given notice. See too *Lakatamia Shipping Company Limited v Morimoto* [2019] EWCA Civ 2203.

(h) Ancillary orders.

Replace n.580 with:

18-089 580 CPR r.25.1(1)(g); *A v C* [1981] Q.B. 956n.; *AJ Bekhor & Co Ltd v Bilton* [1981] Q.B. 923; *Z Ltd v A-Z* [1982] Q.B. 558; *JSC Mezhdunarodniy Promyshlenniy Bank v Pugachev* [2015] EWCA Civ 139; [2015] W.T.L.R. 991. It is important that the court give practical effect to the freezing order to ensure its efficacy: *JSC BTA Bank v Ablyazov (No.7)* [2011] EWCA Civ 1386; [2012] 1 W.L.R. 1988; *Khrapunov v JSC BTA Bank* [2018] EWCA Civ 819. The court has jurisdiction to require a party to sign a mandate to social media and email providers, authorising them to disclose details of their accounts to the other party and to a court-appointed independent lawyer: *Lakatamia Shipping Co Ltd v Su* [2020] EWHC 865 (Comm); [2020] 1 W.L.R. 2852.

7. Anti-suit Injunctions

(b) Foreign proceedings.

Replace n.618 with:

18-094 618 *Deutsche Bank v Highland Crusader Offshore Partners LP* [2009] EWCA Civ 725; [2010] 1 W.L.R. 1023 at [50]. See too *Joint Stock Asset Management Co Ingosstrakh-Investments v BNP Paribas SA* [2012] EWCA Civ 644; [2012] 1 Lloyd's Rep. 649; *SAS Institute Inc v World Programming Ltd* [2020] EWCA Civ 599.

Replace n.626 with:

626 Brussels I Regulation (recast) (1215/2012), which replaced Brussels I Regulation (44/2001) in January 2015; *Turner v Grovit* [2004] E.C.R. I-3565; [2005] 1 A.C. 101. However, this Regulation only seeks to update, and maintain continuity with, the Brussels Convention: Recital 19 to the Preamble; *West Tankers Inc v Allianz SpA* [2009] 1 A.C. 1138; [2009] 3 W.L.R. 696 (ECJ) at [28]. For the view that the *West Tankers* decision should no longer be followed, see the opinion of AG Wathelet in *Gazprom OAO* (C-536/13) [2015] I.L.Pr. 31 which was not endorsed in the judgment of the CJEU. This Regulation applies during the "transition period", but not once EU law no longer applies in the UK after 11pm on 31 December 2020 (see European Union (Withdrawal Agreement) Act 2020 s.39(1)) and UK regulations have already been made to revoke the Brussels I Regulation (recast) from that date: SI 2019/479 Pts 2 and 3. These UK regulations would make important amendments to both primary and secondary legislation, notably the Civil Jurisdiction and Judgments Act 1982. At the time of writing, the UK Government has formally requested to join the Lugano Convention, but it is not known whether that request will be accepted.

Replace third paragraph with:

The English court does have the power to restrain either the commencement or continuation of foreign proceedings in a court outside the European Union.[629] Such an order may restrain a person from prosecuting proceedings in a foreign court[630] or from enforcing a judgment obtained abroad.[631] Historically, relief was available where the foreign proceedings were vexatious and oppressive,[632] or where an order had been obtained in breach of contract or by fraud.[633] The principles upon which relief is now granted may be summarised as follows[634]: (i) the court has the power to restrain a defendant over whom it has personal jurisdiction from instituting or continuing proceedings in a foreign court when it is necessary in the interests of justice to do so; (ii) the English court must have a sufficient interest to protect in restraining the foreign proceedings[635]; (iii) injunctive relief may still be available where the proceedings before the foreign court are vexatious or oppressive[636]; (iii) the order is not an order against the foreign tribunal but, rather, an order against the parties; (iv) the prosecution of parallel proceedings in different jurisdictions is undesirable but not necessarily vexatious or oppressive; (v) since the effect of an order is to affect the conduct of litigation abroad, the jurisdiction should be exercised with caution.

[629] *Donohue v Armco Inc* [2001] UKHL 64; *Royal Bank of Scotland Plc v Hicks* [2010] EWHC 2579 (Ch) and [2011] EWHC 287 (Ch).

[630] *Settlement Corp v Hochschild* [1966] Ch. 10.

[631] *Ellerman Lines Ltd v Read* [1928] 2 K.B. 144. For further examples of "anti-enforcement" injunction see, e.g. *Bank St Petersburg v Arkhangelsky* [2014] EWCA Civ 593; [2014] 1 W.L.R. 4360; *Ecobank Transnational Inc v Tanoh* [2015] EWCA Civ 1309; [2016] 1 W.L.R. 2231; *SAS Institute Inc v World Programming Ltd* [2020] EWCA Civ 599.

[632] *McHenry v Lewis* (1882) 22 Ch. D. 397; *Cohen v Rothfield* [1919] 1 K.B. 410; *Orr-Lewis v Orr-Lewis* [1949] P. 347.

[633] *Ellerman Lines Ltd v Read* [1928] 2 K.B. 144.

[634] See, e.g. *Albon (t/a NA Carriage Co) v Naza Motor Trading Sdn Bhd* [2007] EWCA Civ 1124; [2008] 1 All E.R. (Comm) 351; *Glencore International AG v Exeter Shipping Ltd* [2002] EWCA Civ 528; [2002] 2 All E.R. (Comm) 1; *Masri v Consolidated Contractors International Co Sal* [2008] EWCA Civ 625; [2009] Q.B. 503.

[635] For an example of a court issuing an anti-suit injunction in order to protect its jurisdiction under s.5 of Regulation (EU) 1215/2012, [2012] O.J. L351/1 on jurisdiction (known as "Brussels I (recast)"), see *Petter v EMC Europe Ltd* [2015] EWCA Civ 828. On art.4(1) of the Regulation see *Gray v Hurley* [2019] EWCA Civ 2222; [2020] 1 F.L.R. 864 (referred to CJEU).

[636] Foreign proceedings brought in breach of an exclusive jurisdiction or arbitration agreement are usually so considered. See e.g. *Bank St Petersburg v Arkhangelsky* [2014] EWCA Civ 593. However, the threshold of "vexatious and oppressive" is not easy to meet: see *Star Reefers Inc v JFC Group Co Ltd* [2012] EWCA Civ 14; [2012] 2 All E.R. (Comm) 225, in which Rix LJ (at [2]) thought the test was analogous to that employed to determine an abuse of process (*Aktas v Adepta* [2010] EWCA Civ 1170; [2011] 2 W.L.R. 945).

(c)   Arbitrations.

Replace n.679 with:

[679] *Aggeliki Charis Compania Maritima SA v Pagnan SpA, The Angelic Grace* [1995] 1 Lloyd's Rep. **18-095** 87. This was supported in *Ust-Kamenogorsk Hydropower Plant JSC v AES Ust-Kamenogorsk Hydropower Plant LLP* [2013] UKSC 35; [2013] 1 W.L.R. 1889, in which the Supreme Court also emphasised that s.44 of the Arbitration Act 1996 does not restrict the power of the Court to grant an injunction, under the Senior Courts Act 1981 s.37, to protect a party's contractual right to arbitration in circumstances in which arbitral proceedings are not even pending (provided that the court proceedings in question were not in a jurisdiction within the scope of the Brussels Regulation or Lugano Convention). See also *Western Bulk Shipowning III A/S v Carbofer Maritime Trading ApS* [2012] EWHC 1224 (Comm); [2013] 2 Lloyd's Rep. 163; *Bannai v Erez* [2013] EWHC 3689 (Comm); [2014] B.P.I.R. 4; *Emmott v Michael Wilson & Partners* [2018] EWCA Civ 51. Similar principles apply to a third party to the contract containing the arbitration clause: *Shipowners' Mutual Protection and Indemnity Association (Luxembourg) v Containerships Denizcilik Nakliyat Ve Ticaret A.S. ("Yusuf Cepnioglu")* [2016] EWCA Civ 386; [2016] 3 All E.R. 697; *Qingdao Huiquan Shipping Company v Shanghai Dong He Xin Industry Group Co Ltd* [2018] EWHC 3009 (Comm); [2019] 1 Lloyd's Rep. 520. The Court of Justice of the European Union has confirmed that an anti-suit injunction awarded by an EU-seated arbitral tribunal is not incompatible with the Brussels Regulation: *Gazprom OAO* (C-536/13) [2015] I.L.Pr. 31. For discussion concerning the correct approach to determining the proper law of an arbitration agreement see *Enka Insaat ve Sanayi AS v OOO Insurance Co Chubb* [2020] EWCA Civ 574 (judgment of an appeal to the Supreme Court is pending).

Replace n.640 with:

[640] Arbitration Act 1996 s.32 and s.72. Challenges to an award on the basis of substantive jurisdiction are governed by s.67; *Nori Holding Ltd v Public Joint-Stock Co Bank Otkritie Financial Corp* [2018]

EWHC 1343 (Comm); [2018] 2 Lloyd's Rep. 80. See too *Minister of Finance (Inc) v International Petroleum Investment Co* [2019] EWCA Civ 2080; [2020] Bus. L.R. 45.

CHAPTER 19.

RECEIVERS

5. RECEIVER BY WAY OF EQUITABLE EXECUTION

1. General

Replace para.19-026 with:

A judgment creditor normally obtained satisfaction of its judgment by execu- **19-026**
tion at common law, using the writ of fieri facias, attachment of debts and, in the
case of land, the writ of *elegit*.[151] There were cases, however, where the creditor
could not levy execution at law owing to the nature of the property, the principal
case being where the property was merely equitable, such as an interest under a trust
or an equity of redemption.[152] In order to meet this difficulty, the Court of Chancery
evolved a process of enforcement by way of appointing a receiver of the judgment
debtor's interest.[153]

151 The writ of *elegit* was abolished in 1956 by the Administration of Justice Act 1956 s.34(1), and replaced by the system of charging orders now found in the Charging Orders Act 1979. At the same time, the court was empowered by what is now the Senior Courts Act 1981 s.37(4) to appoint a receiver by way of equitable execution over legal estates and interests in land whether or not a charging order has been obtained.

152 *Anglo-Italian Bank v Davies* (1878) 9 Ch. D. 275.

153 *Re Shephard* (1889) 43 Ch. D. 131; *Anglo-Italian Bank v Davies* (1878) 9 Ch. D. 275.

After the first paragraph, add new para.19-026A:

19-026A By the Judicature Act 1873 the power to appoint a receiver was put on a statutory footing and made available to all divisions of the High Court.[154] The power now contained in the Senior Courts Act 1981 s.37 may be exercised whenever it appears to the court to be "just and convenient" to do so. Notwithstanding the breadth of this language, for a long time the courts considered that the power could only be exercised in circumstances in which the Court of Chancery would have appointed a receiver before the Judicature reforms.[155] In *Parker v London Borough of Camden*, however, Sir John Donaldson MR said he did not accept that the practices of the Court of Chancery "still rule us from their graves".[156] Eventually, in *Masri (No.2)*,[157] the Court of Appeal held that the statutory power is not constrained by reference to pre-1873 practice. Instead, the circumstances in which receivers may be appointed in aid of enforcement may be developed incrementally, applying old principles to new situations. *Masri (No.2)* has been forcefully affirmed by the Privy Council.[158] These decisions substantially enlarge the potential scope and utility of the remedy.

154 Judicature Act 1873 s.25(8).

155 *Holmes v Millage* [1893] 1 Q.B. 551 CA; *Edwards & Co v Picard* [1909] 2 K.B. 903; *Harris v Beauchamp Bros* [1894] 1 Q.B. 801 CA; *Morgan v Hart* [1914] 2 K.B. 183 CA; *Maclaine Watson & Co Ltd v International Tin Council* [1988] Ch. 1 aff'd [1989] Ch. 253 CA

156 *Parker v London Borough of Camden* [1986] Ch. 162 CA 173.

157 *Masri v Consolidated Contractors International (UK) Ltd (No 2)* [2009] Q.B. 450 CA.

158 *Tasarruf Mevduati Sigorta Fonu v Merrill Lynch Bank and Trust Co (Cayman) Ltd* [2012] 1 W.L.R. 1721 PC. The Supreme Court of Ireland has followed the same path: *ACC Loan Management Limited DAC v Rickard* [2019] IESC 29.

2. Land

Replace para.19-027 with:

19-027 [This sub-section is deleted in the supplement.]

3. Property not Available for Execution

Replace para.19-028 with:

19-028 [This sub-section is deleted in the supplement.]

After the third sub-section, add new sub-section:

3A. Scope and exercise of the jurisdiction

19-029 Until *Masri (No.2)* it was sometimes thought that there was only jurisdiction to appoint a receiver over an asset which would be presently amenable to execution by normal means if only the judgment debtor held the legal interest instead of a mere equitable interest.[159] That is now seen to be an outdated practice rather than a jurisdictional limit. In considering the scope of the jurisdiction, and in exercising that jurisdiction,[160] the demands of justice are the overriding consideration.[161] These include promotion of a policy that English judgments and awards should be complied with and, if necessary, enforced.[162]

The jurisdiction will not be exercised unless there is some hindrance or difficulty in using the normal processes of execution, which may be legal or practical.[163] The classical legal hindrance was the inability of common law execution to reach an equitable interest, but it is no longer necessary that the hindrance should arise out of the nature of the property. Practical difficulties may include steps taken by the judgment debtor to put assets beyond reach in order to frustrate enforcement as well as the holding of assets through multiple chains of companies rendering enforcement complex.[164] The courts are realistic about the difficulties a judgment creditor may face executing overseas against a recalcitrant judgment debtor.[165] It is not necessary to show that execution by other means would be impossible or even very difficult.[166] Receivership may be justified, for example, where it is likely to result in a greater recovery by facilitating the sale of a business as a going concern.[167]

A receiver will not be appointed if the court is satisfied that the appointment **19-030** would be fruitless, for example because there is no property that the receiver can get in.[168] It is enough, however, that there is a reasonable prospect that the appointment will be of practical utility in the enforcement of a judgment or award.[169]

The appointment should not be disproportionate and the court may consider less onerous alternatives.[170] In considering whether to make the appointment, the court should have regard to the amount claimed by the judgment creditor, the amount likely to be received by the receiver, and the probable costs of the appointment.[171]

[159] E.g. *Holmes v Millage* [1893] 1 QB 551 CA 555. But cf. *Maclaine Watson & Co v International Tin Council* [1988] Ch. 1 at 19-21.

[160] *Tasarruf Mevduati Sigorta Fonu v Merrill Lynch Bank and Trust Co (Cayman) Ltd* [2012] 1 W.L.R. 1721 PC at [56].

[161] E.g. *JSC VTB Bank v Skurikhin* [2015] EWHC 2131 (Comm) [53].

[162] *Cruz City 1 Mauritius Holdings v Unitech Ltd* [2015] 1 All E.R. (Comm) 336 at [47(a)].

[163] *Cruz City 1 Mauritius Holdings v Unitech Ltd* [2015] 1 All E.R. (Comm) 336 at [47(c)]. CPR 69PD 4.1(3) requires that the written evidence supporting the application give details of "why the judgment cannot be enforced by any other method", as to which see *VB Football Assets v Blackpool Football Club (Properties) Ltd* [2019] B.C.C. 896 at [13]-[14].

[164] *Cruz City 1 Mauritius Holdings v Unitech Ltd* [2015] 1 All E.R. (Comm) 336.

[165] *Masri v Consolidated Contractors International Company SAL* [2008] EWHC 2492 (Comm) at [18].

[166] *Masri v Consolidated Contractors International Company SAL* [2008] EWHC 2492 (Comm) at [17].

[167] *VB Football Assets v Blackpool Football Club (Properties) Ltd* [2019] B.C.C. 896 at [15]-[20].

[168] *Manchester & Liverpool District Banking Co Ltd v Parkinson* (1888) 22 Q.B.D. 173; *Morgan v Hart* [1914] 2 K.B. 183; *Maclaine Watson & Co Ltd v International Tin Council* [1988] Ch. 1 (on appeal, see [1989] Ch. 253 at 271); *Bourne v Colodense Ltd* [1985] I.C.R. 291 CA at 302.

[169] *Cruz City 1 Mauritius Holdings v Unitech Ltd* [2015] 1 All E.R. (Comm) 336 at [47(e)].

[170] *JSC VTB Bank v Skurikhin* [2015] EWHC 2131 (Comm) at [56]; *Blight v Brewster* [2012] 1 W.L.R. 2841 at [75]-[76] (where it was more convenient to empower the judgment creditor's solicitor to make the election in question on behalf of the judgment debtor).

[171] CPR 69PD 5.

After the third sub-section, add new sub-section:

3B.   The nature of the relief

19-031   The remedy does not involve "execution" in the ordinary sense of the word, but is a form of equitable relief given in substitution for execution.[172] An application to appoint a receiver is not an action on a judgment to which the Limitation Act 1980 s.24 applies.[173]

The receiver is authorised to receive the assets over which the appointment is made. As such, a third party's payment of an English debt to the receiver will discharge the judgment debtor's claim,[174] and a third party who knows of the receivership will not be discharged if instead they pay the judgment debtor. The receiver will commonly be authorised to take steps to recover the assets, exercising the judgment debtor's rights, including taking legal proceedings against third parties.[175] Amongst other things, a receiver may be authorised to exercise the judgment debtor's rights as a shareholder,[176] under a pension scheme,[177] or as settlor of a revocable trust.[178] The order may give the receiver a power of sale,[179] and a receiver may apply to the court to approve a particular transaction.[180]

19-032   The receiver's appointment also takes effect as an injunction restraining the judgment debtor from receiving any part of the assets it covers.[181] In consequence, third parties who know of the order will be in contempt of court if they transfer assets to the judgment debtor or otherwise assist in frustrating the receivership.

The court may make such ancillary orders against the judgment debtor as are appropriate in the circumstances to further the purposes of the receivership. For example, the court may require that the judgment debtor not dispose of assets or otherwise deal with them prejudicially to the judgment creditor[182]; or take whatever steps are necessary to transfer assets or powers to the receiver[183]; or provide information about assets[184]; or confirm the receiver's authority and entitlements to third parties.[185]

The appointment of a receiver by way of equitable execution does not have any proprietary effect such as would operate in rem to determine property rights against the world at large.[186] That is, the order itself does not vest any property in the receiver, create an equitable charge, or give the judgment creditor priority over other creditors.

[172]   *Re Shepherd* (1889) 43 Ch. D. 131 CA; *Norburn v Norburn* [1894] 1 Q.B. 448.

[173]   *Behbehani v Behbehani* [2020] 1 F.C.R 603 CA at [81].

[174]   *Masri v Consolidated Contractors International (UK) Ltd (No. 2)* [2009] Q.B. 450 CA at [55]. Whether payment to a receiver of a foreign debt discharges the debt depends on the applicable law of the contract.

[175]   *Masri v Consolidated Contractors International (UK) Ltd (No.2)* [2009] Q.B. 450 CA at [22]. The order in that case provided that the receiver could either sue in the name of the judgment debtor or in its own name.

[176]   *Cruz City 1 Mauritius Holdings v Unitech Ltd* [2015] 1 All E.R. (Comm) 336 at [48].

[177]   *Blight v Brewster* [2012] 1 W.L.R. 2841 at [76].

[178]   *Tasarruf Mevduati Sigorta Fonu v Merrill Lynch Bank and Trust Co (Cayman) Ltd* [2012] 1 W.L.R. 1721 PC.

[179]   E.g. *JSC BTA Bank v Ablyazov* [2013] EWHC 1361 (Comm).

[180]   *VB Football Assets v Blackpool Football Club (Properties) Ltd* [2019] 4 W.L.R. 93.

[181]   *Masri v Consolidated Contractors International (UK) Ltd (No.2)* [2009] Q.B. 450 CA at [53]; *Stevens v Hutchinson* [1953] Ch. 299 at 305; *Re Sartoris's Estate* [1892] 1 Ch. 11 CA 12.

[182] *Re Marquis of Anglesey* [1903] 2 Ch. 727; *Lloyd's Bank v Medway Upper Navigation Co* [1905] 2 K.B. 359.

[183] *Tasarruf Mevduati Sigorta Fonu v Merrill Lynch Bank and Trust Co (Cayman) Ltd* [2012] 1 W.L.R. 1721 PC at [61]; *Blight v Brewster* [2012] 1 W.L.R. 2841 at [76].

[184] E.g. *Masri v Consolidated Contractors International (UK) Ltd (No.2)* [2009] Q.B. 450 CA at [23], [28], [183]. The order is helpfully appended to the Court of Appeal's judgment.

[185] E.g. *Masri v Consolidated Contractors International (UK) Ltd (N.2)* [2009] Q.B. 450 CA at [23], [28].

[186] *Masri v Consolidated Contractors International (UK) Ltd (No.2)* [2009] Q.B. 450 CA at [53]-[58], [71]; *JSC VTB Bank v Skurikhin* [2019] EWHC 1407 (Comm) [71]; *Re Potts Ex p Taylor* [1893] 1 QB 648 CA.

After the third sub-section, add new sub-section:

3C.   Assets amenable to equitable execution

It has been said that a receiver by way of equitable execution may be appointed **19-033** over whatever may be considered in equity as the assets of the judgment debtor,[187] but this seems too narrow. Certainly the classical case is where the judgment debtor has an equitable interest that cannot be reached by legal execution, such as a non-discretionary interest under a trust[188] or an equity of redemption.[189] But the remedy is available more widely:

(a)   A receiver may be appointed over assets which the judgment debtor owns absolutely, provided only that there is some hindrance or difficulty in using the normal processes of execution. Assets located outside England are one example.[190] Another is a claim to be indemnified by a third party which is not an attachable debt.[191]

(b)   A receiver may be appointed where there is, for the time being at least, no asset at all, as in the case of future debts[192] or, in an Irish case, future entitlements under a statutory scheme.[193]

(c)   Finally, a receiver may be appointed to exercise a power where this would result in assets vesting in the judgment debtor, such as a settlor's power to revoke a trust.[194] Lord Collins has said that the settlor's rights in such a case are "tantamount to ownership",[195] but this is confusing because the settlor does not have any interest, equitable or otherwise, in any asset until the power is exercised.[196]

[187] *Tasarruf Mevduati Sigorta Fonu v Merrill Lynch Bank and Trust Co (Cayman) Ltd* [2012] 1 W.L.R. 1721 PC at [6].

[188] *Webb v Stanton* (1883) 11 Q.B.D. 518 CA. A pure discretionary beneficiary of a trust has no proprietary interest and receivers cannot be appointed in terms that compel a trustee to exercise the discretion in favour of such a beneficiary. Similarly, de facto control over assets, in the sense that there is a practical likelihood that the holder would act on the judgment debtor' instruction, but no obligation on them to do so, is insufficient. See *JSC VTB Bank v Skurikhin* [2019] EWHC 1407 (Comm) [102]-[109].

[189] *Anglo-Italian Bank v Davies* (1878) 9 Ch. D. 275 CA.

[190] As in *Masri v Consolidated Contractors International (UK) Ltd (No.2)* [2009] Q.B. 450 CA itself.

[191] *Bourne v Colodense Ltd* [1985] I.C.R. 291 CA; *Maclaine Watson & Co Ltd v International Tin Council* [1988] Ch. 1 at 19-21 (Millett J) aff'd [1989] Ch. 253 CA.

[192] *Masri v Consolidated Contractors International (UK) Ltd (No.2)* [2009] Q.B. 450 CA; and see *Soinco SACI v Novokuznetsk Aluminium Plant* [1998] Q.B. 406. In *Holmes v Millage* [1893] 1 Q.B. 551 the Court of Appeal held that equitable execution cannot be used to in relation to future earnings, but they are now regulated by the Attachment of Earnings Act 1971.

[193] *ACC Loan Management Limited DAC v Rickard* [2019] IESC 29.

194 *Quaere* whether a receiver may also be appointed to exercise a beneficiary's power to terminate a trust using the power recognised in *Saunders v Vauthier* (1841) Cr. & Ph. 240.

195 *Tasarruf Mevduati Sigorta Fonu v Merrill Lynch Bank and Trust Co (Cayman) Ltd* [2012] 1 W.L.R. 1721 PC at [59].

196 Smith, *"Execution against a power of revocation"* (2013) 129 L.Q.R. 332.

After the third sub-section, add new sub-section:

3D.   Assets outside the jurisdiction

19-034   Because the order does not affect title, but operates in personam, there is no rule preventing the court from making a receivership order by way of equitable execution in relation to foreign assets, provided the court has personal jurisdiction over the judgment debtor and subject matter jurisdiction in relation to the assets.[197] It is not a bar to the appointment of receivers that the English court's order will not or may not be recognised by the foreign court where the assets are located.[198] If the foreign court will not enforce the English court's order, including by recognising the receiver's authority, the order will still regulate the judgment debtor's conduct,[199] and their non-compliance may be sanctioned by contempt proceedings in England. Where assets are located outside England it will usually be appropriate to include in the order modified Babanaft provisos making clear that non-party foreigners are not affected by the order except to the extent it is enforced by a foreign court.[200]

197 *Masri v Consolidated Contractors International (UK) Ltd (No.2)* [2009] Q.B. 450 CA at [50]-[58]; *Cruz City 1 Mauritius Holdings v Unitech Ltd* [2015] 1 All E.R. (Comm.) 336 at [35].

198 *Derby & Co Ltd v Weldon (Nos 3 & 4)* [1990] Ch. 65 CA at 86; *Derby & Co Ltd v Weldon (No.6)* [1990] 1 W.L.R. 1139 CA at 1150; *Masri v Consolidated Contractors International (UK) Ltd (No.2)* [2009] Q.B. 450 CA at [69].

199 In general, the order should not require the judgment debtor to do something which exposes it to a real danger of criminal liability under the law of its home state or the state where the assets are located: *Masri v Consolidated Contractors International Company SAL* [2008] EWHC 2492 (Comm) at [26]; *Cruz City 1 Mauritius Holdings v Unitech Ltd* [2015] 1 All E.R. (Comm) 336 at [39].

200 *Masri v Consolidated Contractors International (UK) Ltd (No.2)* [2009] Q.B. 450 CA at [61], [71]; *Taurus Petroleum Ltd v State Oil Marketing Co of the Ministry of Oil, Iraq* [2016] 1 Lloyd's Rep. 42 CA at [33]-[37]; *Babanaft International Co SA v Bassatne* [1990] Ch. 13 CA.

CHAPTER 20.

PERSONAL MONETARY CLAIMS

2.   ACCOUNTING IN EQUITY

2.   Accountability for Funds

Replace n.14 with:

[14] *John v Dodwell and Co* [1918] A.C. 563 PC at 569 ("a transmitted fiduciary obligation to ac-   **20-013**
count"); *British America Elevator Co Ltd v Bank of British North America* [1919] A.C. 658 PC at 663–
64; *Arthur v AG of Turks & Caicos Islands* [2012] UKPC 30 at [37]; and see Mitchell and Watterson,
"Remedies for Knowing Receipt" in Mitchell (ed), *Constructive and Resulting Trusts* (2010) and PG
Turner, "Accountability for profits derived from involvement in breach of fiduciary duty" [2018] CLJ
255.

(a) Proceedings for general accounts.

(1) The right to an account.

After "the court's findings.", add:

20-015 The claimant must also prove that an account has not been provided or is inadequate.[21a]

[21a] *Ball v Ball* [2020] EWHC 1020 (Ch) [22].

Replace second paragraph with:

Since the Judicature reforms the court has enjoyed a discretion whether to order a general accounting even once the requisite relationship is proved. The court will ordinarily order an account where none has been given,[22] especially in cases involving conventional trusts,[22a] but it may refuse relief where the effect of the reversal of the onus of proof would be "to enable the plaintiff to blackmail the defendant",[23] or where an account is unnecessary or disproportionate or premature or unlikely to be fruitful.[24] The court may need to have regard to the information that has already been provided, any difficulties the accounting party may now face, and the motivation for seeking an account.[25] It may be appropriate to order an account only of particular assets or transactions.

[22] *Henchley v Thompson* [2017] W.T.L.R. 1289 at [25], [60]; *Al-Dowaison v Al-Salam* [2019] EWHC 301 (Ch) at [148].

[22a] *Ball v Ball* [2020] EWHC 1020 (Ch) [21], distinguishing commercial cases, where an accounting may only have practical utility if it may lead to a financial claim.

[23] *Campbell v Gillespie* [1900] 1 Ch. 225, at 229.

[24] *Libertarian Investments Ltd v Hall* [2014] 1 H.K.C. 368 (CFA) at [172]; *Henchley v Thompson* [2017] W.T.L.R. 1289 (citing a predecessor of this passage).

[25] *Al-Dowaison v Al-Salam* [2019] EWHC 301 (Ch) at [150]–[152].

(3) Taking the account.

Replace first paragraph with:

20-017 What information and documents an accounting party must provide depends on the circumstances and should be considered at the hearing. The essential requirement is the account must say what the assets were, what has been done with them, what the assets now are, and what distributions have taken place.[32a] The account must inform and where necessary explain. Depending on the case, the beneficiaries may therefore be entitled to sufficient material to enable them to understand the movements on the account, the nature of the investments, the monies expended and recovered; the income earned; the expenses paid; and how, and when and on what basis investment decisions were made.[33] In some cases this may require formal trust accounts but in other cases less formal documents may suffice or a narrative explanation may be required.[34]

[32a] *Ball v Ball* [2020] EWHC 1020 (Ch) [24], [58].

[33] *Best v Ghose* [2018] IEHC 376 at [92]–[97].

[34] *Royal National Lifeboat Institution v Hedley* [2016] EWHC 1948 (Ch) at [11]; *Ball v Ball* [2020] EWHC 1020 (Ch).

(7) Misapplications.

Replace third paragraph with:

However, in *Target Holdings Ltd v Redferns*,[65] the House of Lords held that, at **20-021** least in the case of a non-traditional commercial trust, a trustee should not be required to reconstitute a trust from which they have misapplied assets where the same loss (in the sense of abstract harm) would have occurred if the trust had been performed in accordance with its terms. This controversial decision was thought by many to confuse the liability of trustees to pay reparative compensation for losses caused by a breach of trust with their liability to account for the trust property.[66] However, in *AIB Group (UK) Plc v Mark Redler & Co Solicitors*,[67] the Supreme Court declined to reconsider the approach adopted in *Target Holdings Ltd v Redferns*, and indeed extended the approach to traditional trusts. According to the court, the basic model is that the trustee must restore the trust fund to the financial position it would have occupied if the trustee had performed his obligation. Foreseeability of loss is irrelevant, but compensation should not exceed the loss caused by the breach of trust, in the sense that the loss must flow directly from the breach.[68] This decision has not been well received in all quarters[69] and it is clear from subsequent cases that important issues remain to be considered.[69a]

[65] *Target Holdings Ltd v Redferns* [1996] 1 A.C. 421 at 434.

[66] See, e.g. Millett (1998) 114 L.Q.R. 214.

[67] *AIB Group (UK) Plc v Mark Redler & Co Solicitors* [2015] A.C. 1503.

[68] See also *Barnett v Creggy* [2017] 2 W.L.R. 1054 CA, per Sales LJ at [45].

[69] Critics include Millett (2018) 32 Trust LI 44; Gummow (2015) 41 *Australian Bar Review* 5; Watts [2015] L.M.C.L.Q. 118; Lee (2015) 9 *Journal of Equity* 94; Shaw-Mellors [2015] J.B.L. 165; Edelman, Penner and Ho in Degeling and Varuhas (eds), *Equitable Compensation and Disgorgement of Profits* (2017).

[69a] See especially *Main v Giambrone & Law (a firm)* [2018] P.N.L.R. 2 CA; *Interactive Technology Corp Ltd v Ferster* [2018] EWCA Civ 1594; and *Auden McKenzie (Pharma Division) Limited v Patel* [2020] B.C.C. 316 CA.

(b)   Accounts on the footing of wilful default.

(1)   Wilful default.

Replace n.75 with:

[75] *Re Owens* (1882) 47 L.T. 61 CA; *Shah v Shah* [2020] EWHC 1840 (Ch) [76] (citing this paragraph);   **20-024** and see Stannard [1979] Conv. 345.

(4)   Surcharge for wilful default.

After "that never materialised.", add new n.90a:

[90a] For example *Sim Poh Ping v Winsta Holding Pte Ltd* [2020] SGCA 35 at [120].   **20-027**

3.   EQUITABLE COMPENSATION

Replace n.93 with:

[93] *Bristol and West Building Society v Mothew* [1998] Ch. 1 CA at 17; *Libertarian Investments Ltd v*   **20-028** *Hall* [2014] 1 H.K.C. 368 (CFA) at [168] and [170]; *Agricultural Land Management Ltd v Jackson (No.2)* [2014] WASC 102 at [334]–[375]; *Interactive Technology Corp Ltd v Ferster* [2018] EWCA Civ 1594; *Zhang Hong Liv DBS Bank (Hong Kong) Limited* [2019] HKCFA 45; *Sim Poh Ping v Winsta Holding Pte Ltd* [2020] SGCA 35 (a particularly valuable discussion).

1. Reparative Compensation

Change title of para.20-033 to:

(d) Dishonest assistance.[110]

20-033 [110] See Ch.30 and Elliott and Mitchell (2004) 67 M.L.R. 16.

2. Substitutive Compensation

Replace para.20-035 with:

20-035 For instance, this concept applies where upon the specific performance of a contract, a vendor is obliged to pay compensation for defects in the asset,[113] and also where upon rescission a party cannot return an asset in specie or cannot return it in the same condition.[114] Classically, where a custodial fiduciary had misapplied assets, on the taking of their account they would be charged with the value of the asset.[115] Their personal liability to pay this amount, conventionally labelled compensation,[116] involved an obligation to perform their duties in respect of the asset substitutively and the compensation was a substitute for the missing asset. However, the effect of *AIB Group (UK) Plc v Mark Redler & Co Solicitors* has been to superimpose an essentially reparative model of liability in this situation to the extent that liability should not exceed the loss that would have occurred if the trustee had done his duty.[117] The extent and limits of this ruling remain unclear. In the most recent decision, *Auden McKenzie (Pharma Division) Limited v Patel,*[117a] the Court of Appeal indicated that liability to restore a payment made by directors of a company in breach of fiduciary duty should not be limited by reference to the (assumed) fact that if the company had not made that payment, it could and would have made a payment of the same amount to the same recipient but in a lawful manner.

[113] See section 6 below.

[114] See section 5 below.

[115] See section 2(a)(7) above.

[116] This is sometimes called "restitution" or "restoration", e.g. *Re Paycheck Services 3 Ltd* [2011] Bus L.R. 111 HL at [48], where Lord Hope contrasted this remedy with "damages or equitable compensation", meaning reparative compensation; and *Ahmed v Ingram* [2018] B.P.I.R. 535 CA at [34].

[117] *AIB Group (UK) Plc v Mark Redler & Co Solicitors* [2015] A.C. 1503.

[117a] *Auden McKenzie (Pharma Division) Limited v Patel* [2020] B.C.C. 316 CA.

4. ACCOUNT OF PROFITS

1. Nature of Relief

Replace para.20-037 with:

20-037 Relief given by way of an account of profits is measured by the gain made by the wrongdoer irrespective of whether the claimant has suffered a corresponding loss.[119] On the taking of the account, the object is "to determine as accurately as possible the true measure of the profit or benefit obtained".[120] Typically, the court must determine the sums impermissibly received and deduct any allowable expenses.[120a] An account of profits therefore proceeds on a different principle from reparative compensatory damages or equitable compensation. The principle is also different from that which regulates awards of damages on the user basis, where the claimant is compensated for the invasion of their rights by an award reflecting the price at which they might have licensed the relaxation of their right in a hypothetical negotiation.[121] Those damages also deprive the defendant of a gain but it is of a different type to the gain to be disgorged upon an account of profits. The former is, in a sense, objective and the latter, in a sense, subjective. Neither remedy necessarily yields a greater quantum of recovery than the other.[122]

[119] *Attorney General v Blake* [2001] 1 A.C. 268, at 280 (Lord Nicholls); *Murad v Al-Saraj* [2005] W.T.L.R. 1573 CA at [67].

[120] *Warman International Ltd v Dwyer* (1995) 182 C.L.R. 544 at 588; *Re Jarvis* [1958] 1 W.L.R. 815 at 820.

[120a] In an intellectual property context, see *Lifestyle Equities CV v Santa Monica Polo Club Limited* [2020] EWHC 688 (Ch) [59] and, in relation to the allowable expenses, *OOO Abbott v Design and Display Ltd* [2017] F.S.R. 43 (IPEC) [57].

[121] As to this distinction and awards on the user basis, see amongst others *Attorney General v Blake* [2001] 1 A.C. 268; *Experience Hendrix LLC v PPX Enterprises Inc* [2003] 1 All E.R. (Comm) 830 CA; *WWF—World Wide Fund for Nature v World Wrestling Federation Entertainment Inc* [2007] Bus L.R. 1252 CA; *Devenish Nutrition Ltd v Sanofi-Aventis SA* [2009] Ch. 390 CA; *Pell Frischmann Engineering Ltd v Bow Valley Iran Ltd* [2011] 1 W.L.R. 2370 PC. Awards of this nature may be made in equity, particularly in relation to breaches of confidence, as to which see Ch.9; but also in the context of trusts, as to which see *Tang Man Sit v Capacious Investments Ltd* [1996] A.C. 514 PC at 522; and Edelman and Elliott (2004) 18 T.L.I. 116.

[122] *FHR European Ventures LLP v Cedar Capital Partners LLC* [2015] A.C. 250. The question whether the claimant may elect between personal and proprietary remedies, and the date at which an asset should be valued for the purposes of the personal remedy, were discussed in *Global Energy Horizons Corp v Gray* [2015] EWHC 2232 (Ch) at [128]–[144].

Replace n.123 with:

[123] *FHR European Ventures LLP v Cedar Capital Partners LLC* [2015] A.C. 250..   **20-038**

2.   Availability

(b)   Accessories.

Replace para.20-041 with:

Those who assist dishonestly in a breach of trust or of fiduciary duty, and appar-   **20-041** ently those who knowingly receive trust property,[128] may also be required to account for profits they gain as a result.[129] The remedy is more restricted than that available against a fiduciary. First, an accessory will only be accountable for profits they gain as a sufficiently direct causal result of their misconduct, so that even profits they would not otherwise have gained may be excluded from the account if the misconduct was not their effective cause.[130] Secondly, the court has a discretion to withhold the remedy if, for example, it would be disproportionate.[131] A dishonest assistant is not accountable for profits gained by the primary wrongdoer.[132]

[128] *Ultraframe (UK) Ltd v Fielding* [2005] EWHC 1638 (Ch) at [1577]; and, in Australia, *Grimaldi v Chameleon Mining NL (No.2)* [2012] FCAFC 6 at [253], [555]. See also *Akita Holdings Ltd v Attorney General of the Turks and Caicos Islands* [2017] A.C. 590 (PC –TCI), which, although put on the basis the company was a knowing recipient, may be better explained on the basis the company was the wrongdoing fiduciary's vehicle and accountable jointly with him.

[129] *Novoship (UK) Ltd v Nikitin* [2015] Q.B. 499 CA confirming a line of first instance authority. The case did not involve a knowing recipient but the Court indicated (at [80]) that the same remedy is in principle available. See generally Elliott and Mitchell "Remedies for Dishonest Assistance" (2004) 67 M.L.R. 17; and Mitchell and Watterson, "Remedies for Knowing Receipt" in Mitchell (ed), *Constructive and Resulting Trusts* (2010); Glister, "Accounts of Profits and Third Parties" in Degeling and Varuhas (eds), *Equitable Compensation and Disgorgement of Profit* (2017).

[130] *Novoship (UK) Ltd v Nikitin* [2015] Q.B. 499 CA at [94]–[115]. See also the High Court of Australia's discussion of related issues in *Ancient Order of Foresters in Victoria Friendly Society Ltd v Lifeplan Australia Friendly Society Ltd* (2018) 360 A.L.R. 1, noted by Ridge (2019) J Eq 69.

[131] *Novoship (UK) Ltd v Nikitin* [2015] Q.B. 499 CA at [119].

¹³² *Ultraframe (UK) Ltd v Fielding* [2005] EWHC 1638 (Ch) at [1595]–[1601]; *Novoship (UK) Ltd v Mikhaylyuk* [2012] EWHC 3586 (Comm) [99]; *Electrosteel Castings (UK) Ltd v Metalpol Ltd* [2014] EWHC 2017 (Ch) at [50]–[51]. This proposition has been treated as also applicable where defendants are jointly and severally liable for infringements of intellectual property: *Lifestyle Equities CV v Santa Monica Polo Club Limited* [2020] EWHC 688 (Ch) [35].

(e) Torts

Replace n.150 with:

20-044   ¹⁵⁰ *Forsyth-Grant v Allen* [2008] Env L.R. 41 CA. In *Coventry v Lawrence* [2014] A.C. 822 the Supreme Court left open the possibility of damages assessed by reference to the benefit to the defendant of not suffering an injunction.

6.   MONETARY AWARDS RELATING TO SPECIFIC PERFORMANCE AND INJUNCTIONS

1.   Damages Under Lord Cairns' Act

20-058   *Change title of para.20-058:*

(a)   Lord Cairns' Act.

(b)   Scope of the jurisdiction.

Replace para.20-058 with:

20-059   The principal object of Lord Cairns' Act was to enable the Court of Chancery, when declining to grant equitable relief and leaving the plaintiff to their remedy at law, to award the plaintiff damages itself instead of sending them to the common law courts to obtain that alternative relief.¹⁸⁹ The merger of jurisdictions brought about by the Judicature Act 1873 had the consequence that any division of the High Court may now award both specific relief and damages in the same proceedings so that the power to award damages in addition to other relief has lost its significance.¹⁸⁹ᵃ The power to award damages in substitution for other relief turned out, however, to have been a substantive innovation with lasting consequences¹⁹⁰ Under this rubric the courts may award damages in two circumstances in which damages were previously not given by any court. First, Lord Cairns' Act created a power to award damages for breach of certain purely equitable rights, such as a covenant running with the land only in equity.¹⁹¹ Secondly, Lord Cairns' Act created a power to give relief in certain cases where a cause of action has not yet accrued. Damages are recoverable at common law only in respect of causes of action which are complete at the date of the claim form; damages for future or repeated wrongs must be made the subject of fresh proceedings. Damages in substitution for an injunction, however, may encompass prospective loss resulting from continuing infringement¹⁹² and indeed damages may be given in substitution for a quia timet injunction where the wrong has only been threatened.¹⁹³ Similarly, damages for breach of contract may be given under Lord Cairns' Act in substitution for specific performance even though the claim form preceded completion so that there was not yet a breach.¹⁹⁴

¹⁸⁹ *Ferguson v Wilson* (1866) L.R. 2 Ch. App. 77, 88.

¹⁸⁹ᵃ Senior Courts Act 1981 s.49; *Morris-Garner v One Step (Support) Ltd* [2019] A.C. 649 at [43].

¹⁹⁰ Reynolds argues that this was a wrong turn: (2019) 13 J Eq 46.

¹⁹¹ *Eastwood v Lever* (1863) 4 De G.J. & S. 114, 46 E.R. 859 CA; *Wrotham Park Estate Co v Parkside Homes Ltd* [1974] 1 W.L.R. 798 is a more recent example.

¹⁹² *Bracewell v Appleby* [1975] Ch. 408; *Jaggard v Sawyer* [1995] 1 W.L.R. 269 CA.

[193] *Leeds Industrial Co-operative Society Ltd v Slack* [1924] A.C. 851; *Hooper v Rogers* [1975] Ch. 43 CA

[194] *Hasham v Zenab* [1960] A.C. 316; *Oakacre Ltd v Claire Cleaners (Holdings) Ltd* [1982] Ch. 197.

Change title of para.20-060: **20-060**

(c) Availability of the jurisdiction.

Replace first paragraph with:

The power arises whenever the court "has jurisdiction to entertain an application" for an injunction or specific performance. This question must be determined as at the date of the claim form.[195] If the court would then have had jurisdiction to grant an injunction or specific performance, it has jurisdiction to award damages instead. But when the court comes to consider whether to grant specific relief or to award damages instead, it must do so by reference to the circumstances as they exist at the date of the hearing.

[195] *Ferguson v Wilson* (1866) 2 Ch. App. 77 at 91; *Johnson v Agnew* [1980] A.C. 367; *Morris-Garner v One Step (Support) Ltd* [2019] A.C. 649 at [45].

Replace second paragraph with:

Whether the court has jurisdiction to award damages under Lord Cairns' Act depends on whether, at the date of the claim form, the court *could* (however unwisely) have granted specific relief, not whether it *would* have done so.[197] Jurisdiction will therefore be declined if, at the date of the claim form, it was impossible to grant specific relief.[198] Damages may, however, be awarded if there is jurisdiction to give specific relief but it is refused on some discretionary ground[199] such as laches,[200] acquiescence[201] or mistake,[202] or if a grant of specific relief would for some reason be inappropriate.[203] Burrows argues that the essential question is whether the claimant had an arguable case for specific relief when the proceedings began.[203a]

[197] *City of London Brewery Co v Tennant* (1873) L.R. 9 Ch. App. 212; *Hooper v Rogers* [1975] Ch. 43 at 48; *Pell Frischmann Engineering Ltd v Bow Valley Iran Ltd* [2011] 1 W.L.R. 2370 PC at [48] and [54], Lord Walker said that equitable damages can be given even if the claimant had no prospect of being granted an injunction, but Lord Sumption doubted this in *Morris-Garner v One Step (Support) Ltd* [2019] A.C. 649 at [113].

[198] *Lavery v Pursell* (1888) 39 Ch. D. 508 (lapse of time); *Rogers v Challis* (1859) 27 Beav. 175 (contract to borrow money); *Hipgrave v Case* (1885) 28 Ch. D. 356 (performance impossible because of sale of land by claimant to a third party); *Proctor v Bayley* (1889) 42 Ch. D. 390 (no threat to continue the wrong).

[199] *Wroth v Tyler* [1974] Ch. 30; *Price v Strange* [1978] Ch. 337 at 358–360, 368–370.

[200] *McKenna v Richey* [1950] V.L.R. 360; and see *Eastwood v Lever* (1863) 4 De G.J. & S. 114; *Senior v Pawson* (1866) L.R. 3 Eq. 330; *Sayers v Collyer* (1884) 24 Ch. D. 103, all cases on refusal of injunctions.

[201] *Gafford v Graham* [1999] 41 E.G. 159.

[202] *Dell v Beasley* [1959] N.Z.L.R. 89.

[203] *Tito v Waddell (No.2)* [1977] Ch. 106 at 321–323, 325–328 (damages instead of replanting of trees over a small number of isolated plots). But in an appropriate case the reason which lead the court to refuse specific performance may also lead it to refuse to make an order for damages in substitution thereof: *Gafford v Graham* [1999] 41 E.G. 159 (injunction refused on basis of acquiescence).

[203a] Burrows, *Remedies for Torts, Breach of Contract, and Equitable Wrongs* (4th edn 2019) 315-316.

Replace third paragraph with:

Where the claimant seeks specific relief, the court may award damages under Lord Cairns' Act even though damages was not included in the prayer.[204] Equally, it has been said that a claimant who is content to receive damages under Lord

Cairns' Act is entitled to say so in terms, and does not have to make the pretence of seeking non-monetary relief,[205] but this has been doubted.[205a]

[204] See *Betts v Neilson* (1868) L.R. 3 Ch. App. 429 at 441.

[205] *Pell Frischmann Engineering Ltd v Bow Valley Iran Ltd* [2011] 1 W.L.R. 2370 PC at [48]; *Jaggard v Sawyer* [1995] 1 W.L.R. 269 CA at 285.

[205a] *Morris-Garner v One Step (Support) Ltd* [2019] A.C. 649 at [45] (Lord Reed) and Burrows, *Remedies for Torts, Breach of Contract, and Equitable Wrongs* (4th edn 2019) 315-316.

(d) Damages in substitution for injunctions.

Replace para.20-061 with:

20-061   The court can properly award damages "once and for all" in respect of future infringements because it awards them in substitution for an injunction and to compensate for those future wrongs which an injunction would have prevented.[206] Since the practical consequence of withholding injunctive relief is to authorise the continuance of an unlawful state of affairs, the doctrine of res judicata operates to prevent the claimant and their successors in title from bringing proceedings thereafter to recover even nominal damages in respect of further wrongs for which the claimant has been fully compensated. For this reason, it has been said that the jurisdiction to award damages in respect of future wrongs (or, rather, the refusal to grant an injunction in respect of such wrongs) should be exercised with caution.[207] On one view, an injunction should not be refused so as to "allow a wrong to continue simply because the wrongdoer is able and willing to pay for the injury he may inflict".[208] However, in *Coventry v Lawrence*[209] the Supreme Court moved away from a mechanical application of the criteria identified in some earlier authorities, at least in cases of nuisance. The decision lies in the unfettered discretion of the court, which is free to take into account, amongst other things, matters of public interest, as well as the effect of a nuisance on third parties.[210] The principles to be applied when considering whether an injunction should be granted are considered in greater detail in Ch.18.

[206] *Attorney General v Blake* [2001] 1 A.C. 268 at 281.

[207] *Shelfer v City of London Electric Lighting Co* [1895] 1 Ch. 287 at 315–316; also *Cowper v Laidler* [1903] 2 Ch. 337 at 341. For examples of the exercise of such caution, see *Kennaway v Thompson* [1981] Q.B. 88 (limited injunction granted); and *Tetley v Chitty* [1986] 1 All E.R. 663 (damages insufficient remedy).

[208] *Shelfer v City of London Electric Lighting Co* [1895] 1 Ch. 287 at 315, 316; applied in *Kelsen v Imperial Tobacco Co (of Great Britain and Ireland) Ltd* [1957] 2 Q.B. 334.

[209] *Coventry v Lawrence* [2014] A.C. 822.

[210] See especially para.18-044.

(f) Measure of damages.

Replace first paragraph with:

20-063   In *Johnson v Agnew*, Lord Wilberforce said he found in Lord Cairns' Act "no warrant for the court awarding damages differently from common law damages".[211] In *Morris-Garner v One Step (Support) Ltd*, Lord Reed, speaking for a majority of the Supreme Court albeit obiter dicta, indicated that this statement must be read with caution because the measure of damages reflects the special character of the statutory jurisdiction.[212] Damages are said to be given as a monetary substitute for an injunction. They compensate for loss,[213] being the loss the applicant suffers by the refusal of specific relief.[214] However this can be misread. Consistently with earlier cases, what Lord Reed seems to have meant is that damages may be given under the statute as compensation not only for injuries caused by past breaches but also for injuries expected to be caused by future breaches.[214a] Otherwise damages are calculated in the same way in which they would be in a non-statutory case.

[211] *Johnson v Agnew* [1980] A.C. 367 at 400.

[212] *Morris-Garner v One Step (Support) Ltd* [2019] A.C. 649 at [43], [47] and [62]. But compare *Turf Club Auto Emporium Pte Ltd v Yeo Boong Hua* [2018] 2 S.L.R. 655 CA at [286]. The Supreme Court's approach is pointedly criticised by Peel in "Negotiating damages after One Step" (2019) 35 JCL 1.

[213] In *Lunn Poly Ltd v Liverpool & Lancashire Properties Ltd* [2006] 2 E.G.L.R. 29 CA at [22], [24], Neuberger LJ mooted the possibility that within this jurisdiction an account might be given of the profits the defendant had made, is making and will make as a result of the breach, but that is inconsistent with the decision of the Supreme Court in *Morris-Garner v One Step (Support) Ltd* [2019] A.C. 649 at, e.g. [68]–[70], [95(3)]. The Singapore Court of Appeal arrived at the same conclusion in *Turf Club Auto Emporium Pte Ltd v Yeo Boong Hua* [2018] 2 S.L.R. 655 CA at [271].

[214] *Morris-Garner v One Step (Support) Ltd* [2019] A.C. 649 at [44] and [95(3)].

[214a] See *Leeds Industrial Co-operative Society v Slack* [1924] A.C. 851, where Viscount Finlay (at 857 cf. 859) and Lord Dunedin (at 865) both made clear that the damages compensate for the injury caused by the tort (past and future); and *Jaggard v Sawyer* [1995] 1 W.L.R. 269 CA at 276H (Bingham MR) and 286A (Millett LJ), endorsed in *Morris-Garner v One Step (Support) Ltd* [2019] A.C. 649 at [44].

At the end add new paragraph:

In many cases in which Lord Cairns' Act is engaged losses will be justly compensated by an award of negotiating damages, i.e. damages assessed according to the amount which might fairly have been charged for the voluntary relinquishment of the right which the court has declined to enforce, subject to downward adjustment for reasons of fairness.[215] There is a question whether in such cases the fee should be calculated on the basis of what was known to the parties at the date of breach or on the basis of information available up to the time of the judge's decision.[216]

[215] *Morris-Garner v One Step (Support) Ltd* [2019] A.C. 649 at [62] and [95(3)]. See for example *Wrotham Park Estate Co Ltd v Parkside Homes Ltd* [1974] 1 W.L.R. 798; *Bracewell v Appleby* [1975] Ch. 408; *Jaggard v Sawyer* [1995] 1 W.L.R. 269 CA. These are all injunction cases, but in principle such damages might also be awarded in substitution for specific performance, as to which see Millett LJ's dissenting judgment in *Co-operative Insurance Society Ltd v Argyll Stores (Holdings) Ltd* [1996] Ch. 286 CA. In *Coventry v Lawrence* [2014] A.C. 822 the Supreme Court left open the question whether damages assessed on this basis would ever be appropriate in a nuisance case.

[216] *Lunn Poly Ltd v Liverpool & Lancashire Properties Ltd* [2006] 2 E.G.L.R. 29 CA at [23], [29]; *Pell Frischmann Engineering Ltd v Bow Valley Iran Ltd* [2011] 1 W.L.R. 2370 PC at [50]; *Morris-Garner v One Step (Support) Ltd* [2019] A.C. 649 at [56] and [159].

Delete paragraph.

3. Monetary Awards Giving Effect to Specific Performance

(b) Interest.

Replace n.224 with:

[224] For example cl.7.2 of the Standard Conditions of Sale, 5th edn (The Law Society, 2018 revision). **20-070**

7. Accounts Between Co-owners

3. Elements of the Account

(a) Occupation rent.

Replace n.266 with:

[226] *Davis v Jackson* [2017] 1 W.L.R. 4005, discussed in *Shilabeer v Lanceley* [2019] EWHC 3380 (QB) **20-076**

CHAPTER 25.

RESULTING TRUSTS

2. GRATUITOUS TRANSFER

2. Purchase of Property in the Name of Another

(c) Presumption of advancement.

(2) Between parent and child.

Replace n.41 with:

[41] *Hepworth v Hepworth* (1870) L.R. 11 Eq. 10; *Nelson v Nelson* (1995) 184 C.L.R. 538; *Laskar v Laskar* [2008] EWCA Civ 347; [2008] 1 W.L.R. 2695 (presumption of some weight between mother and adult child but rebutted by direct evidence); *Re Watkin (a bankrupt), Wood v Watkin* [2019] EWHC 1311 (Ch).   **25-009**

CHAPTER 27

APPOINTMENT, RETIREMENT AND REMOVAL OF TRUSTEES

CONTENTS

1. CAPACITY TO BE A TRUSTEE

At the start of the paragraph, replace "Two" with:

27-001   Three

1. Corporations

(b)   Trust corporations.

Replace n.11 with:

27-003   [11] TA 1925 s.68(1)(18); LPA 1925 s.205(1)(xxviii); SLA 1925 s.117(1)(xxx); LP(Am)A 1926 s.3 (extending the definitions in the former Acts). Certain individuals such as trustees in bankruptcy and trustees under deeds of arrangement are also comprised in the term "trust corporation".

After para.27-004, add new sub-section:

3. Non-Residents

27-004A   There is no general rule that prevents a settlor from appointing a person resident abroad as trustee of a trust established in England. Where the appointment is made by a person with the power to appoint a new trustee, or by the court, then it is only in exceptional circumstances that a person resident abroad can be appointed trustee.[21a] Exceptional circumstances include those where the beneficiaries are resident abroad, where it is likely to be for their benefit to have trustees appointed in the same jurisdiction.[21b]

[21a] *Re Whitehead's Will Trusts* [1971] 1 W.L.R. 833.

[21b] *Richard v Mackay* [2008] W.T.L.R. 1667

2. NUMBER OF TRUSTEES

Following para.27-004A add new sub-section at the beginning:

A1.   General rule

27-004B   Although settlors commonly stipulate that at least two trustees are required in order to exercise the trust powers, in the absence of an express provision the general rule is that there is no minimum number of trustees. Trusts with sole trustees are not normally considered to be desirable given the risk of fraudulent behaviour. Furthermore, sole trustees, except in the case of a trust corporation, cannot give valid receipt for the sale proceeds from land.[21c] There is no general rule that limits the number of trustees, and a trust deed may require any number of trustees to act. However, in light of the normal rule that trustees must act unanimously[21d] there are obvious risks to the appointment of too many trustees.

[21c] See LPA 1925 s.27(2); SLA 1925 ss.18(1), 94; TA 1925 ss.14, 37. cf. SCA 1981 s.114 as to personal representatives (para.31-021).]

[21d] *Luke v South Kensington Hotel Co* (1879) 11 Ch 121.

1.   Land

Replace para.27-005 with:

27-005   Where a settlement of land or a trust of land is created, the number of trustees must not exceed four; and if more than four trustees are named, the first four named who are able and willing to act will alone be the trustees.[22] This rule does not apply in the following cases[23]:

(i)   where land, or the proceeds of sale of land, is held in trust for charitable, ecclesiastical or public purposes;

(ii) a term of years limited by a settlement on trusts for raising money, e.g. portions; or

(iii) a term of years created under the statutory remedies for enforcing rentcharges.[25]

[22] TA 1925 s.34(1). cf. SCA 1981 s.114, replacing JA 1925 s.160; considered in *In b Holland* (1936) 105 L.J.P. 113 as to the number of personal representatives. Before 1926 there was no such restriction; for the relevant transitional provisions, see TA 1925 s.34(2).). For difficulties where there is a conveyance to the partners of a firm and there are more than four such partners, see: *Vanquish Properties (UK) Ltd v Brook Street (UK) Ltd* [2016] EWHC 1508.

[23] TA 1925 s.34(3).

[25] The Rentcharges Act 1977 prohibits the creation of new rentcharges.

2.   Exceptions

Replace para.27-006 with:
[This sub-section is deleted in the supplement.]   **27-006**

3.   APPOINTMENT OF TRUSTEES

After the first sub-section, add new sub-section:

1A.   Trustee's Consent

A person cannot be compelled to act as a trustee, and an intended trustee must **27-007A** accept the office of trusteeship.[28a] Acceptance may be express, as where a trustee signs the declaration of trust[28b] or inferred from their conduct, such as their taking steps in the administration of the trust.[28c] Where an intended trustee has not accepted the office, he is free to disclaim.[28d] The disclaimer may be express, or it may be implied from conduct inconsistent with trusteeship.[28e] The consequences of disclaimer depend upon the circumstances. Where there is a conveyance to several trustees, and one of their number disclaims, the fund will vest in the non-disclaiming trustees, who shall be free to exercise the rights and powers of trusteeship without the concurrence of the disclaiming trustee.[28e] Where there is a conveyance to a sole trustee who disclaims (or to several trustees who all disclaim), the disclaiming trustee is not subject to the liabilities, duties and powers of trusteeship.[28f] Their sole duty is to reconvey the fund to the settlor, who will receive it subject to the originally declared trusts. Where the trust is established by will, and the intended trustees disclaim, the fund remains vested in the personal representatives who may either appoint new trustees or administer the trusts themselves.[28g]

[28a] *Re Sharman's Will Trusts* [1942] Ch. 311 at 314; and see generally on disclaimer *Re Stratton's Disclaimer* [1958] Ch. 42 (beneficial gift by will).

[28b] *Ong v Ping* [2015] EWHC 1742, [98].

[28c] *James v Frearson* (1840) 1 Y & Coll Ch 370; *In re Stevens* [1897] 1 Ch. 432.

[28d] *Mallott v Wilson* [1903] 2 Ch 494. A disclaimer of an interest under a will before the death of the testator is ineffective: *Smith v Smith (Disclaimer of Interest under will)* [2001] 3 All E.R. 552.

[28e] *Stacey v Elph* (1833) 1 M & K 195 (purchase of trust property); *Re Clout and Frewer's Contract* [1924] 2 Ch. 230 (inaction for a long period after declaration of trust); but see *Re Birchall* (1889) 40 Ch. D. 436.

[28e] *Nicholson v Wordsworth* (1818) 2 Swan 365.

[28f] *Mallott v Wilson* [1903] 2 Ch 494.

[28g] *Re Cockburn's Will Trusts* [1957] Ch 438.

2. Initial Trustees

Replace para.27-008 with:

27-008 Normally the first trustees are appointed by the will or settlement. Unless and until new trustees are appointed, the property remains vested in the first trustees (or such of them as do not retire and are not removed[31]), and when one dies, the trust property devolves upon the survivors. On the death of a sole or sole surviving trustee, the trust property, whether real or personal, vests in his personal representatives, still subject to the trust.[32] Until new trustees are appointed, the personal representatives, though they are not bound to accept the position and duties of trustees,[33] are capable of exercising or performing any power or trust which the deceased trustee could have exercised or performed, unless the trust instrument (if any) contains a contrary direction.[34]

[31] See paras 27–033 to 27–036.

[32] AEA 1925 ss.1 and 3 replacing CA 1881 s.30.

[33] *Re Benett* [1906] 1 Ch. 216.

[34] TA 1925 s.18(2) replacing CA 1911 s.8(1). See P.W. Smith (1977) 41 Conv. (NS) 423 for the position where personal representatives die without appointing new trustees.

3. Subsequent Trustees

Replace para.27-009 with:

27-009 [This sub-section is deleted in the supplement.]

4. Appointment of New Trustees

(b) The Trustee Act 1925.

(1) The power.

Replace list item "(viii)" with:

27-012 (viii) He is removed under a power in the trust instrument.[50]

[50] TA 1925 s.36(2). *Re Gleeds Retirement Benefit Scheme* [2015] Ch. 212 (no requirement for a deed, as writing is sufficient).

(2) The appointment.

Replace list item "(ii)" with:

27-013 (ii) By the surviving or continuing trustees or trustee. This includes a refusing or retiring trustee, if willing to make the appointment, but not a trustee removed against his will.[63] If there is no such trustee, the appointment may be made—[64]

[63] *Re Stoneham's Settlement Trusts* [1953] Ch. 59.

[64] TA 1925 s.36(8); *Rettendon Parish Council v Hart* [2020] EWHC 2221 (trustee appointed for a fixed term does not 'retire' on expiry of term, and therefore cannot exercise the power).

(3) The person appointed.

Replace para.27-014 with:

27-014 It is expressly provided that the person making the appointment may appoint himself.[74] He should not, however, appoint anyone whom the court would not appoint,[75] although the appointment is not necessarily invalid if he does,[76] nor, if he is a trustee, is such an appointment itself a breach of trust.[77] But if the appointor is a minor, the appointment will be closely scrutinised, and may be set aside.[78]

[74] TA 1925 s.36(1), altering on this point TA 1893 s.10; see *Re Sampson* [1906] 1 Ch. 435. Compare the position under express powers (para.27-011) and contrast the power of appointing additional trustees (para.27-016).

[75] See para.27-019.

[76] *Forster v Abraham* (1874) L.R. 17 Eq. 351 (tenant for life); *Re Earl of Stamford* [1896] 1 Ch. 288 (solicitor to tenant for life); *Re Coode* (1913) 108 L.T. 94 (husband of tenant for life); and see *Re Cotter* [1915] 1 Ch. 307.

[77] *Briggs v Parsloe* [1937] 3 All E.R. 831.

[78] *Re Parsons* [1940] Ch. 973; quaere what this case decided: see (1941) 57 L.Q.R. 25.

(d)   The court.

(1)   Trustee Act 1925.

Replace n.96 with:

[96] TA 1925 s.41, replacing TA 1893 s.25.   **27-018**

Delete sub-paragraph "Judicial Trustees Act 1896.".   **27-020**

Delete sub-paragraph "Public Trustee Act 1906.".   **27-021**

4.   VESTING OF TRUST PROPERTY

2.   Exceptions

After "transferring such property.", add new footnote 129a:
[129a] *Re AMT Coffee Ltd* [2018] EWHC 1562.   **27-023**

5.   THE PUBLIC TRUSTEE

After para.27-024 add new paragraph:

The title of this section should be changed to: Statutory Trustees
There are three trustees that are creations of statute that require special men-   **27-024A**
tion, namely the judicial trustee, custodian trustees, and the Public Trustee. Whereas judicial trustees and custodian trustees are types of trusteeship that can be held by any appropriate person, the Public Trustee is a corporation sole.[131] The use of statutory trustees, although less common in recent times, is often desirable in cases where it has proved difficult to find appropriate persons to act as normal trustees, or where there has been breakdown in relationship between the trustees and beneficiaries.

[131] Public Trustee Act 1906 s.1.

1.   Appointment and Powers

Replace para.27-025 with:
[This sub-section is deleted in the supplement.]   **27-025**

2.   Limits to Powers

Replace para.27-026 with:
[This sub-section is deleted in the supplement.]   **27-026**

27-027   *Change title of sub-section:*

3.   As Custodian Trustee

Replace para.27-027 with:
[This sub-section is deleted in the supplement.]

After the third sub-section, add new sub-section:

3A.   The Judicial Trustee

27-027A   **(a)   General**   Judicial Trustees Act 1896[132] created the role of the 'judicial trustee'. A judicial trustee has the same powers of a normal trustee, but is appointed by and acts under the control of the court. The object of the Act:

> "was to provide a middle course in cases where the administration of the estate by the ordinary trustees had broken down and it was not desired to put the estate to the expense of a full administration"

by the court.[133] Until recently the Act offered the only way of replacing a personal representative once a grant had been made and he had begun the administration.[134] The jurisdiction is commonly resorted to where, for reasons not necessarily involving fault on the part of the representative (e.g. illness or conflicting interest), it is expedient to replace him.

27-027B   **(b)   Appointment**   On an application by the settlor or a trustee or a beneficiary, the court may appoint any fit and proper person nominated in the application,[135] or an official of the court (usually the Official Solicitor), to be a judicial trustee to act alone or jointly[136] with any other person and, if sufficient cause is shown, in place of all or any existing trustees. The Act allows the court to appoint a judicial trustee to be a Settled Land Act trustee,[137] or to administer the estate of a testator or intestate instead of the executor or administrator,[138] though not to administer part of the estate, since an executorship is indivisible.[139] In all cases the appointment of a judicial trustee is absolutely discretionary.[140]

27-027C   **(c)   Powers of the judicial trustee**   A judicial trustee differs from an ordinary trustee in a number of respects. He is an officer of the court, and as such is subject to its control and supervision; he can at any time obtain the court's directions as to the way in which he is to act, without the necessity of a formal application; he is entitled to such remuneration as the court allows him; every year he must prepare accounts for examination by the court,[141] although a corporate trustee[142] need only submit such accounts to such persons as the court directs[143]; and he cannot appoint a successor under the statutory power[144] for this would usurp the function of the court.[145] In other respects he is in the position of any other trustee, and so, for example, he can compromise claims.[146]

[132] Judicial Trustees Act 1896 s.1; and see Judicial Trustee Rules 1983 (SI 1983/370), replacing with amendments Judicial Trustee Rules 1972 (SI 1972/1096).

[133] *Re Ridsdel* [1947] Ch. 597 at 605, per Jenkins J.

[134] See now Administration of Justice Act 1985 s.50 (power of court to appoint substitute for, or remove, personal representative), para.34-015.

[135] See *Douglas v Bolam* [1900] 2 Ch. 749.

[136] It is not, however, desirable for a judicial trustee and a private trustee to hold office jointly: *Re Martin* [1900] W.N. 129.

[137] *Re Marshall's Will Trusts* [1945] Ch. 217.

[138] *Re Ratcliff* [1898] 2 Ch. 352.

[139] *Re Wells* [1968] 1 W.L.R. 44.

[140] *Re Ratcliff* [1898] 2 Ch. 352.

[141] Judicial Trustee Rules 1983 rr.9, 10, 12. A yearly audit was formerly required: Judicial Trustees Act 1896 s.1(6), partially repealed by Administration of Justice Act 1982 s.75(1) and Sch.9 Pt I.

[142] Judicial Trustee Rules 1983 r.2(1).

[143] Judicial Trustee Rules 1983 r.13.

[144] TA 1925 s.36, above.

[145] *Re Johnston* (1911) 105 L.T. 701.

[146] *Re Ridsdel* [1947] Ch. 597; for the power of compromise, see para.28-026.

4. As Ordinary Trustee

Replace para.27-028 with:

[This sub-section is deleted in the supplement.]   **27-028**

After the fourth sub-section, add new sub-section:

4A. Custodian Trustees

(a) General The role of custodian trustee was created by the Public Trustee Act **27-028A**
1906.[147] A custodian trustee is appointed along with other trustees known as the 'management trustees'. Whereas the management trustees are responsible for the active management and administration of the trust, the custodian trustee has custody of the trust fund and trust documents.[148] The various bodies who may act as a custodian trustee are prescribed by the rules made under the Public Trustee Act,[149] and include the Public Trustee, the Treasury Solicitor, particular corporations, health authorities, local authorities and other public bodies. A custodian trustee may be appointed by a settlor, anyone with the power to appoint a trustee, or the court.[150]

(b) Powers of the custodian trustee When appointed, the trust property must **27-028B**
be transferred to the custodian trustee as if he were sole trustee,[151] and all the securities and documents of title relating to the trust property are to be in his sole custody. Further, all sums payable to or out of the income of the trust property are to be paid to or by him, except that he may allow the dividends and other income to be paid to the other trustees (called the "managing trustees"), or as they may direct. The management of the trust property and the exercise of any power or discretion exercisable by the trustees under the trust remain vested in the managing trustees.[152] Where there is a power to appoint new trustees, this is exercisable by the managing trustees, although the custodian trustee has the power to apply to the court for the appointment of a new trustee.[153] The court has power to determine a custodian trusteeship if it is expedient,[154] e.g. when it is desirable for the trustee to become an ordinary trustee.[155]

[147] Public Trustee Act 1906 s.4(1). See generally S. G. Maurice (1960) 24 Conv. (N.S.) 196.

[148] Public Trustee Act 1906 s.4(2).

[149] Public Trustee Rules 1912 r.30 (as amended).

[150] Public Trustee Act 1906 s.4(1).

[151] Public Trustee Act 1906 s.4(2)(a)-(c).

[152] Public Trustee Act 1906 s.4(2)(b).

[153] Public Trustee Act 1906 s.4(2)(f).

[154] Public Trustee Act 1906 s.4.

[155] *Re Squires Settlement* (1945) 115 L.J.Ch. 90.

5. As Personal Representative

Replace para.27-029 with:

27-029 [This sub-section is deleted in the supplement.]

After the fifth sub-section, add new sub-section:

5A. The Public Trustee

27-029A **(a)** **General** The office of the Public Trustee was established by the Public Trustee Act 1906. The purpose of the Public Trustee was to act in cases where it was otherwise difficult to find a person willing to act as trustee. The chief advantages derived from appointing him to act as a trustee are as follows. First, being a corporation sole, the office has perpetual existence, despite the death or retirement of the individual from time to time holding it; secondly, the Lord Chancellor's Department is responsible for any loss to the trust estate caused by his breaches of trust[156]; and thirdly, he has a wide experience in trust matters, and yet his fees are moderate. He may, if he thinks fit, act as a custodian trustee, as an ordinary trustee, or as a judicial trustee, and may act alone or jointly with another person or other persons[157]; and he may hold land.[158]

27-029B **(b)** **Limits to Powers** The Public Trustee may decline to accept any trust, and the current practice is that he only accepts trusts as a matter of last resort. However, the Public Trustee must not decline solely on the ground of the smallness of the trust property.[159] Further, he cannot accept any trust exclusively for religious or charitable purposes,[160] nor any except an English trust[160a], nor any trust under a deed of arrangement for the benefit of creditors; nor can he undertake the administration of any estate known or believed by him to be insolvent. He also, as ordinary trustee, cannot carry on a business without the leave of the Treasury, unless he is satisfied that it can be carried on without risk of loss, and he carries it on:

    (i) for not more than 18 months; and
    (ii) with a view to sale, disposition, or winding up.

27-029C **(c)** **As Custodian Trustee** The Public Trustee may be appointed to act as custodian trustee may be made by the court, or by the settlor, or by the person who has power to appoint new trustees. When so appointed, the Public Trustee has the same powers and duties of a normal custodian trustee.[160b]

27-029D **(d)** **As Ordinary Trustee** The Public Trustee may be appointed to be an ordinary trustee, either as an original or a new trustee or as an additional trustee, in the same cases and in the same manner and by the same persons or court as if he were a private trustee; and even if the trustees originally appointed were two or more, the Public Trustee may be appointed sole trustee.[160c] The Public Trustee may be appointed as sole trustee and exercise all the powers of the trustees under the trust despite a direction in the trust instrument that on appointment of new trustees the number shall not be reduced below three[160d] and despite a direction that no discretion vested in the trustees may be exercised at any time when there are less than two trustees.[160e] But if the trust instrument prohibits his appointment he may not be appointed a new or additional trustee unless the court otherwise orders.[160f] Further, if it is proposed to appoint him as a new or additional trustee, notice must be given to the beneficiaries; and on the application of any beneficiary, the court may prohibit the appointment if it considers it expedient to do so having regard to the interests of all the beneficiaries.[160g]

(e) As Personal Representative The Public Trustee is also given power to obtain probate of a will or letters of administration.[160h] Further, with the leave of the court an executor who has obtained probate, or an administrator who has obtained letters of administration, may transfer to the Public Trustee the whole future administration of the estate, and in that way escape all liability in respect of the further administration.[160i] **27-029E**

[156] Under s.7 of the Public Trustee Act 1906 the liability was that of the Consolidated Fund. Section 7 was repealed by Public Trustee (Liability and Fees) Act 2002, with result that the liability is now that of the Lord Chancellor's Department: see 390 HL Official Report (6th series) col.261.

[157] Public Trustee Act 1906 s.2.

[158] *Re Leslie's Hassop Estates* [1911] 1 Ch. 611.

[159] Public Trustee Act 1906 s.2(3).

[160] See *Re Hampton* (1919) 88 L.J.Ch. 103. See para.23-064 for the Official Custodian for Charities.

[160a] *Re Hewitts Settlement* [1915] 1 Ch. 228.

[160b] See above.

[160c] Public Trustee Act 1906 s.5(1).

[160d] *Re Moxon* [1916] 2 Ch. 595.

[160e] *Re Duxbury's Settlement Trusts* [1995] 1 W.L.R. 425.

[160f] Public Trustee Act 1906 s.5(3).

[160g] Public Trustee Act 1906 s.5(4); see *Re Firth (No.1)* [1912] 1 Ch. 806.

[160h] Public Trustee Act 1906 s.6(1); Public Trustee Rules 1912 r.6.

[160i] Public Trustee Act 1906 s.6(2).

6. DETERMINATION OF TRUSTEESHIP

1. Disclaimer

Replace para.27-030 with:
[This sub-section is deleted in the supplement.] **27-030**

Delete para.27-031 "Limits to disclaimer.". **27-031**

Delete para.27-032 "Effect on property.". **27-032**

4. Removal

Replace para.27-036 with:
The statutory power to remove a trustee under s.41 of the Trustee Act 1925 is not applicable in cases where the claim is brought by someone other than the trustee or beneficiary of the trust.[170a] Furthermore, the statutory power cannot be used for the simple removal of a trustee, where there is not a corresponding appointment of new trustee.[170b] Where the statutory power does not apply, the court has an inherent jurisdiction to remove a trustee (including a trustee of a foreign trust[171]) and to appoint a new one in his place. As the interests of the trust are of paramount **27-036**

importance to the court, this jurisdiction will be exercised whenever the welfare of the beneficiaries requires it,[172] even if the trustees have been guilty of no misconduct.[173] The welfare of the beneficiaries is also the court's guide in exercising its statutory powers of removal, e.g. on bankruptcy.[174] A bankrupt trustee ought to be removed from his trusteeship whenever the nature of the trust is such that he has to receive and deal with trust funds so that he can misappropriate them; but if there is no danger to the trust property, bankruptcy by itself will not necessarily induce the court to remove him.[175]

[170a] s.58(1) TA 1925; *Davidson v Seelig* [2016] EWHC 549 (application by protector refused).

[170b] *London Capital & Finance Plc (in Admin) v Global Security Trustees Ltd* [2019] EWHC 3339 (Ch).

[171] *Chellaram v Chellaram* [1985] Ch. 409.

[172] *Re Wrightson* [1908] 1 Ch. 789; *Miller v Cameron* (1936) 54 C.L.R. 572 (Aus H.C.); *Titterton v Oates* [2001] W.T.L.R. 319 (Australia); *London Capital & Finance Plc (in Admin) v Global Security Trustees Ltd* [2019] EWHC 3339 (Ch) (threshold for the exercise of the inherent jurisdiction is not higher than that of the statutory power).

[173] *Letterstedt v Broers* (1884) 9 App. Cas. 371.

[174] TA 1925 s.41.

[175] *Re Barker's Trusts* (1875) 1 Ch. D. 43; *Re Adam's Trust* (1879) 12 Ch. D. 634.

CHAPTER 30.

BREACH OF TRUST

3. PERSONAL REMEDIES AGAINST THE TRUSTEE IN BREACH

2. Personal Remedies after Breach

(g) Interest and liability for lost income.

Replace first paragraph with:

30-020   The trustee may be liable to pay interest to compensate the trust for losses result-ing from his breach.[79] Where the trustee applies the trust money for his own use, he may also have to account for his unauthorised profit made with the trust money. In principle, the rules for awarding interest should compensate the beneficiary fully for his lost investment returns or make the trustee disgorge his full profit.[80] Where trust money has been misapplied, the court should aim, as far as the evidence reli-ably allows, to award interest which reflects the cost to the trust beneficiaries of be-ing kept out of their money.[81] The exercise of calculating the actual loss to the trust or gain to the trustee may be difficult: it may involve speculative inquiries into the possible income returns on the original capital sum, or the degree to which the trustee's profit was attributable to his use of the trust money. Where however the court has precise and reputable information about the expected returns on the trust investment, then interest should be awarded as a proxy for them.[81a]

[79] e.g. *Stafford v Fiddon* (1857) 23 Beav. 386; *Re Jones* (1883) 49 L.T. 91; *Re Waterman's WT* [1952] 2 All E.R. 1054 (trustee liable for interest representing lost income owing to undue delay in investing trust funds).

[80] S.B. Elliott [2001] Conv. 313 at 319–321.

[81] The principles are summarised in *Challinor v Juliet Bellis & Co* [2013] EWHC 620 (Ch); reversed on other grounds in [2015] EWCA Civ 59; [2016] W.T.L.R. 431; and *Watson v Kea Investments* [2019] EWCA Civ 1759, [2019] 4 W.L.R. 145.

[81a] *Watson v Kea Investments* [2019] EWCA Civ 1759, [2019] 4 W.L.R. 145 at paras [65], [71]-[74.]

Replace third paragraph with:

The special cases where the higher rate may be awarded in a private trust claim are:

(i)   Where the trustee is guilty of fraud or serious misconduct. The higher rate would also be compounded[87] with yearly[88] or even half-yearly rests.[89]

(ii)   Where the trustee has traded with the trust money for his own use. Here he is presumed to have earned more than the standard rate. Interest at the higher commercial rate is available where the beneficiary cannot prove and recover the profits actually made by the trustee with the trust money.[90] Normally compound interest is awarded[91] unless the trading has been for the benefit or partly for the benefit of the beneficiary.[92] Likewise, simple interest would be awarded if the money, while employed in a business or profession, was not used in the normal course of trading.[93]

Alternatively, the court may order an inquiry into the actual loss by the beneficiary owing to the trustee's breach, or the actual rate of return in fact made by the trustee with the trust money (this may include the total return of any investment, includ-ing any capital gain)[93a]:

(i)   thus where the trust claimant can establish what proportion of the trustee's profits was made by trading with the trust money, he must account for that profit rather than pay interest on trust money[94];

(ii)   where a trustee who applied trust money for his own benefit invested it at a rate above the standard trustee rate, he must account for the interest he actually received.[95]

In periods when there is a wide difference between commercial borrowing rates and investment rates, the court may vary from the usual higher rate of one per cent above bank base rate. It may take into account the purpose for which the claimant placed the money on trust with the defendant, and the standard rates of borrowing or investment return that a hypothetical person in the position of the claimant might have expected to pay or receive.[96]

[87] See *Westdeutsche Bank v Islington LBC* [1996] A.C. 669.

[88] See *Re Barclay* [1899] 1 Ch. 674.

[89] *Re Emmet's Estate* (1881) 17 Ch. D. 142. Half-yearly rests are rarely directed: *Burdick v Garrick* (1870) 5 Ch. App. 233.

[90] *Vyse v Foster* (1872) 8 Ch.App. 309 at 329 (affirmed L.R. 7 H.L. 318); *Re Davis, Davis v Davis* [1902] 2 Ch. 314; *Gordon v Gonda* [1955] 1 W.L.R. 885. The beneficiary may not claim the profits of a trader to whom the money has been improperly lent, even though the borrower knew that the money belonged to the trust: *Stroud v Gwyer* (1860) 28 Beav. 130.

[91] *Jones v Foxall* (1852) 15 Beav. 388; *Williams v Powell* (1852) 15 Beav. 461; *Wallersteiner v Moir (No.2)* [1975] Q.B. 373; and see *Westdeutsche Bank v Islington LBC* [1996] A.C. 669.

[92] *O'Sullivan v Management Agency and Music Ltd* [1985] Q.B. 428.

[93] *Burdick v Garrick* (1870) 5 Ch. App. 233.

[93a] *Watson v Kea Investments* [2019] EWCA Civ 1759, [2019] 4 W.L.R. 145.

[94] *Docker v Somes* (1834) 2 My. & K. 655.

[95] *Re Emmet's Estate* (1881) 17 Ch. D. 142.

[96] *Challinor v Juliet Bellis & Co* [2013] EWHC 620 (Ch); reversed on other grounds in [2015] EWCA Civ 59; [2016] W.T.L.R. 43.

4.   Defences and Adjustments to Trustee's Liability

1.   Exemption Clauses and Express Modification of Duty

(b)   Limits on permitted exclusion.

Replace n.116 with:

[116] *Walker v Stones* [2000] 4 All E.R. 412; following *Royal Brunei Airlines Sdn Bhd v Tan* [1995] A.C. 378. See para.30-079 below. An intentional breach of trust that was justifiably committed in the interests of the beneficiaries would not necessarily be dishonest in this sense. "The main duty of a trustee is to commit *judicious* breaches of trust": *Perrins v Bellamy* [1889] 1 Ch. 797, 798 in arg. A trustee who believes her acts are morally justified, or that her actions have not fallen below acceptable standards, may nonetheless be held to have acted dishonestly if an ordinary, honest trustee would not have acted as she did: *Wong v Burt* [2004] NZCA 174; [2005] W.T.L.R. 29; *Barnes v Tomlinson* [2006] EWHC 3115; [2007] W.T.L.R. 377. For the pleading a dishonest breach of trust where the trustee relies on an exoneration clause, see *Sofer v Swiss Independent Trustees SA* [2020] EWCA Civ 699. **30-026**

5.   Proprietary Remedies Against Proceeds of Breach of Trust

3.   Identification and Mixed Funds

(c)   Other contributor innocent.

(2)   Different rules for allocation.

Replace para.30-060 with:
Recent cases have recognised reasons to displace the rule in *Clayton's Case.*   **30-060**

Although it remains the default rule, it may be displaced with relative ease in favour of a solution that produces a fairer result.[261] It would not apply where it was contrary to the actual presumed intentions of the contributors,[262] or was unjust or impractical in its operation.[263] The court may instead treat the mixed fund as subject to a "rolling charge" in favour of each innocent contributor.[264] Debits from the account are borne proportionately by each contributor according to the amount of their money in the account immediately before each withdrawal.[264a] But this approach may become unnecessarily complex or expensive to apply where the mixed fund derives from the deposits of many different contributors made over a long period.[264b] The simpler solution is to treat all withdrawals from the account as borne rateably by all the contributors but to make no adjustment for sequence of deposits and withdrawals from the account.[265] The effect may be to allow a contributor to trace into a withdrawal from the account even though the withdrawal was made before his money had been deposited in the account.

[261] *Charity Commission for England and Wales v Framjee* [2014] EWHC 2507 (Ch); (2014) 17 I.T.E.L.R. 271 at [49].

[262] *Barlow Clowes International Ltd (In Liquidation) v Vaughan* [1992] 4 All E.R. 22; *Russell-Cooke Trust Co v Prentis* [2002] EWHC 2227 (Ch); [2003] All E.R. 478.

[263] *Commerzbank AG v IMB Morgan Plc* [2004] EWHC 2771 (Ch); [2005] 2 All E.R. (Comm) 564.

[264] See *Ontario Securities Commission and Greymac Credit Corp* (1985) 55 O.R. (2d) 673; discussed in *Barlow Clowes International Ltd (In Liquidation) v Vaughan* [1992] 4 All E.R. 22 at 27, 44.

[264a] This applies combines a version of the "lowest intermediate balance" rule in *Roscoe v Winder* [1915] 1 Ch. 62 with the "rolling charge" form of analysis: *Caron v Jahani* [2020] NSWCA 117. See para.30-057 above.

[264b] The authorities and reasons are gathered in *Caron v Jahani* [2020] NSWCA 117 at [106]-[122].

[265] *Barlow Clowes International Ltd (In Liquidation) v Vaughan* [1992] 4 All E.R. 22.

6. PERSONAL LIABILITY OF THIRD PARTIES INVOLVED IN BREACH OF TRUST

4. Dishonest Assistance

(c) Dishonesty.

Replace n.391 with:

30-079   [391] *Royal Brunei Airlines Sdn Bhd v Tan* [1995] 2 A.C. 378, as explained in *Group Seven Ltd v Nasir* [2019] EWCA 614, [2020] Ch 129.

Replace second paragraph with:

When the test of dishonesty is applied, the defendant is not free to be judged according to his own standards. He is judged according the standards of an ordinary honest person, who would have the same knowledge of the circumstances as he does, and sharing some of his personal characteristics, such as his age and experience.[334] His conduct need not be dishonest by the standards of all people, since not all people may appreciate the kinds of specialised wrongdoing involved in certain kinds of commercial transaction.[335] In the past the authorities were uncertain whether the trustee also needed to realise that his conduct would be regarded as dishonest by the standard of an ordinary honest person. The better view, which is now accepted in England, is that the defendant need not also take a view on the propriety of his own conduct.[336] A finding that the defendant was dishonest only involves an assessment of his participation in the impugned transaction, judged in the light of his motives and his knowledge of the facts. Reckless participation in the impugned transaction is not the same as dishonesty unless the defendant's motive for acting was itself dishonest.[337]

[334] *Royal Brunei Airlines Sdn Bhd v Tan* [1995] 2 A.C. 378.

[335] *Starglade Properties Ltd v Nash* [2010] EWCA Civ 314.

[336] Compare the former view in *Twinsectra Ltd v Yardley* [2002] UKHL 165; [2002] 2 A.C. 164 at [32]–[35]; with *Barlow Clowes v Eurotrust International Ltd* [2005] UKPC 37; [2006] 1 All E.R. 333 at [15]–[16]. It is now beyond doubt that the later decision in *Barlow Clowes* case represents the correct view of English law: *Abou-Rahmah v Abacha* [2006] EWCA Civ 1492; [2007] W.T.L.R. 1; *Starglade Properties Ltd v Nash* [2010] EWCA Civ 314; *Group Seven Ltd v Nasir* [2019] EWCA 614, [2020] Ch 129, following *Ivey v Genting Casinos (UK) Ltd (trading as Crockfords Club)* [2017] UKSC 67, [2018] A.C. 391 (restating the corresponding rule in criminal law).

[337] *Clydesdale Bank v Workman* [2016] EWCA Civ 73; [2016] P.N.L.R. 18 at [51].

Replace n.338 with:

[338] *Attorney General of Zambia v Meer Care & Desai (a firm)* [2008] EWCA Civ 1007 at [21]; *Group Seven Ltd v Nasir* [2019] EWCA 614, [2020] Ch 129, at paras [59]-[60].

Replace n.341 with:

[341] *Barlow Clowes v Eurotrust International Ltd* [2005] UKPC 37; [2006] 1 All E.R. 333 at [28], per Lord Hoffmann; *Group Seven Ltd v Nasir* [2019] EWCA 614, [2020] Ch 129, at para [101]-[104].

CHAPTER 37.

CREATION AND SETTING ASIDE OF MORTGAGES

CONTENTS

4. EQUITABLE MORTGAGES

3. **Informal Mortgages**

Replace fourth paragraph with:

37-021   Some decisions suggest that the courts might be willing to give effect to security agreements, notwithstanding a failure to comply with s.2 of the Law of Property (Miscellaneous Provisions) Act 1989, in reliance upon the doctrine of proprietary estoppel.[43] In *Cobbe v Yeoman's Row Management Ltd*, Lord Scott expressed his view that proprietary estoppel could not be used as a means of circumventing s.2, on the basis that equity ought not to contradict a statute by rendering enforceable an agreement that statute has declared to be void where the statute does not contain an express exemption for proprietary estoppel.[44] However, he made clear that this was an obiter comment,[45] and whereas Lord Mance agreed with Lord Scott's speech,[46] Lord Walker expressly considered it unnecessary and inappropriate to consider the issue relating to s.2.[47] Lord Scott's view is analogous to that which obtains where a surety denies the enforceability of a guarantee which does not comply with s.4 of the Statute of Frauds 1677.[48] Consistently with what the House of Lords has held in the surety context,[49] an informal agreement to create a mortgage which does not comply with s.2 ought not, by the mere fact of its existence, to generate a proprietary estoppel in favour of the mortgagee unless there is something further (beyond the mere fact of the mortgagor having agreed orally to create a mortgage) to found that estoppel. But s.2 should not rule out all possibility of an estoppel, if the facts genuinely support it.[50] Facts which might found an estoppel, notwithstanding s.2, could include an express representation that the mortgagor would not rely on the failure to comply with s.2 coupled with detrimental reliance on that representation, or "conscious encouragement"[51] by the mortgagor of the mortgagee's belief that there is a valid contract.[51a] The context within which such representations are made will also be important. *Cobbe v Yeoman's Row* involved commercial parties, who can legitimately be expected to protect themselves by complying with relevant formality requirements,[51b] which may not be the case in other contexts, such as familial relationships.[52] Commercial parties who have expressly negotiated "subject to contract" will not be able to avoid the consequences of taking that approach.[53] Section 2 should also not prevent a valid *Pallant v Morgan* equity[54] from arising, which could generate a constructive trust over property notwithstanding a lack of writing signed by both parties.[55]

[43] *Cobbe v Yeoman's Row Management Ltd* [2005] EWHC 266 (Ch); *Kinane v Mackie-Conteh* [2005] EWCA Civ 45.

[44] *Cobbe v Yeoman's Row Management Ltd* [2008] UKHL 55 at [29]; [2008] 1 W.L.R. 1752.

[45] *Cobbe v Yeoman's Row Management Ltd* [2008] UKHL 55; [2008] 1 W.L.R. 1752.

[46] *Cobbe v Yeoman's Row Management Ltd* [2008] UKHL 55; [2008] 1 W.L.R. 1752 at [96].

[47] *Cobbe v Yeoman's Row Management Ltd* [2008] UKHL 55; [2008] 1 W.L.R. 1752 at [93]. Lord Hoffmann and Lord Brown agreed with the reasons of Lord Scott for allowing the appeal without indicating any view on the s.2 point: at [1] and [94].

[48] See below para.45-009.

[49] See *Actionstrength Ltd v International Glass Engineering IN GL EN SpA* [2003] UKHL 17; [2003] 2 A.C. 541.

[50] *Dowding v Matchmove Ltd* [2016] EWCA Civ 1233; [2017] 1 W.L.R. 749; *Whittaker v Kinnear* [2011] EWHC 1479 (QB) at [30]. See also *Herbert v Doyle* [2010] EWCA Civ 1095, esp. at [57]; *Ely v Robson* [2016] EWCA Civ 774; *Muhammad v ARY Properties Ltd* [2016] EWHC 1698 (Ch); and see the discussion in para.12–046 above; Neuberger, "The Stuffing of Minerva's Owl? Taxomony and Taxidermy in Equity" [2009] C.L.J. 537 at 546; Etherton, "Constructive Trusts and Proprietary Estoppel: The Search for Clarity and Principle" [2009] Conv. 104 at 120. *Kensington Mortgage Co Ltd v Mallon* [2019] EWHC 2512 (Ch) at [149].

[51] Neuberger [2009] C.L.J. 537 at 546.

[51a] For general discussion of the circumstances in which a proprietary estoppel might arise, see ch.12 above, esp. from para.12-032.

[51b] Although the mere fact that an arrangement is a commercial one does not necessarily preclude an estoppel arising: *Kensington Mortgage Co Ltd v Mallon* [2019] EWHC 2512 (Ch) at [144].

[52] See, e.g. *Thorner v Major* [2009] UKHL 18; [2009] 1 W.L.R. 776.

[53] See, e.g. *Generator Developments Ltd v Lidl UK GmbH* [2018] EWCA Civ 396. See also *Farrar v Miller* [2018] EWCA Civ 172 at [46].

[54] *Pallant v Morgan* [1953] Ch. 43.

[55] See s.2(5) of the Law of Property (Miscellaneous Provisions) Act 1989; *Farrar v Miller* [2018] EWCA Civ 172.

8. FORGERIES

Replace n.134 with:

[134] See Land Registration Act 2002 Sch.4. Rectification is not always possible: see paras 3(2) and 6(2) **37-038** of Sch.4. On forgery and alteration of the register, see generally Fox, "Forgery and alteration of the Register under the Land Registration Act 2002" in Cooke (ed), *Modern Studies in Property Law* Vol.3 (Hart Publishing, 2005) Ch.2; and *NRAM Ltd v Evans* [2017] EWCA Civ 1013 at [48]-[59], [2018] 1 W.L.R. 639.

CHAPTER 44.

LIENS

4. SOLICITORS' LIENS

2. Common Law Lien on Property Received Qua Solicitor

(b) Extent of lien.

Replace para.44-018 with:
The lien extends to money paid into a joint account in the names of solicitors for **44-018**

the parties to an action to abide the event of the action.[82] But it is confined to property which has come into the solicitor's hands in his character of solicitor and not otherwise[83]; it does not extend to property which was received by the solicitor in circumstances where the reason for receipt is inconsistent with the existence of a lien[83a] and it is confined to the solicitor's costs, i.e. to items properly included in his bill of costs,[84] and does not include debts.[85] But the lien is a general lien which extends to all costs due from the client, and is not restricted merely to the costs incurred in connection with the property over which the lien is claimed.

[82] *Halvanon Insurance Co Ltd v Central Reinsurance Corp* [1988] 1 W.L.R. 1122.

[83] *Ex p. Fuller* (1881) 16 Ch. D. 617.

[83a] *Withers LLP v Rybak* [2011] EWCA Civ 1419 at [19]-[22], [33] and [51]-[52]; [2012] 1 W.L.R. 1748.

[84] *Re Taylor, Stileman & Underwood* [1891] 1 Ch. 590 at 599.

[85] *Re Galland* (1885) 31 Ch. D. 296.

4. Loss of Lien

(c) Waiver.

Replace para.44-022 with:

44-022   The lien may be discharged by waiver, which will be inferred where the solicitor takes a security for costs which is inconsistent with the solicitor's lien, unless he expressly reserves his lien.[101] The enforcement of a judgment for costs[102] or the taking of security after the solicitor has ceased to act for the client[103] does not lead to the inference that the lien is waived, but a waiver can be inferred from the taking of additional security over the property which would otherwise be covered by the lien, or an acceptance that another creditor's claim to the property will have priority over the solicitor's claim.[103a] The fact that the solicitor has no positive intention to waive the lien does not prevent a waiver from being inferred where the new security arrangement is inconsistent with the lien.[104] The solicitor's duty to explain the combined effect of the new security arrangement and the lien to his or her client means it is easier to infer a waiver of the lien than in other cases, and merely arranging for the client to take independent advice about the terms of the new security arrangement does not enable the solicitor to avoid that duty.[104a]

[101] *Re John Morris* [1908] 1 K.B. 473; *Candey Ltd v Crumpler* [2020] EWCA Civ 26.

[102] *A v B* [1984] 1 All E.R. 265.

[103] *Twigg Farnell v Wildblood* [1998] P.N.L.R. 211.

[103a] *Candey Ltd v Crumpler* [2020] EWCA Civ 26.

[104] *Clifford Harris & Co v Solland International Ltd* [2005] EWHC 141 (Ch) at [40]; [2005] 2 All E.R. 334.

[104a] *Candey Ltd v Crumpler* [2020] EWCA Civ 26 at [56]-[57].

5. Equitable Lien on Property Recovered or Preserved

After "the fund itself.", add:

44-023   The lien may be waived, and waiver can be inferred from the taking of an inconsistent security right.[125a]

[125a] *Candey Ltd v Crumpler* [2020] EWCA Civ 26. See also para.44-022.

6. Statutory Lien on Property Recovered or Preserved

(a) Statutory lien.

After "always have precedence.", add:

The solicitor may also waive the right to apply for a statutory charge, where the solicitor takes an inconsistent security right.[130a] **44-024**

[130a] *Clifford Harris & Co v Solland International Ltd* [2004] EWHC 2488 (Ch) at [15]. See also para.44-022.

INDEX

This index has been prepared using Sweet & Maxwell's Legal Taxonomy. Main index entries conform to keywords provided by the Legal Taxonomy except where references to specific documents or non-standard terms (denoted by quotation marks) have been included. These keywords provide a means of identifying similar concepts in other Sweet & Maxwell publications and on-line services to which keywords from the Legal Taxonomy have been applied. Readers may find some minor differences between terms used in the text and those which appear in the index. Suggestions to *sweetandmaxwell.taxonomy@tr.com*.